# CLIPSTONE CAMP and the MANSFIELD AREA in WORLD WAR ONE

*The impact of a large military presence in a North Nottinghamshire community*

Pauline Marples

Published by
Forest Town Heritage Group 2013

Other books by this author

Forest Town - The Village that Grew Out of Coal
    *The development of a Twentieth Century Nottinghamshire Village*
ISBN 978-0-9551446-0-8

The Forest Town Hostel 1944 - 1959
    by Pauline & Malcolm Marples
ISBN 1-904 102-20-20-4

Published by The Forest Town Heritage Group
email <heritage.foresttown@ntlworld.com>
Copyright Pauline Marples 2013

Printed by
The Nottingham Label Company Limited,
Unit 14 Catton Road, Arnold, Nottingham NG5 7JD

ISBN 978-0-9551446-1-5

*Front cover pictures: Top -Soldiers at Clipstone Camp, centre - Camp Plan - bottom Mansfield Town Hall and Market Square.*

# CONTENTS

# ABBREVIATIONS

NA            Nottingham Archives
TNA          The National Archives formerly PRO Public Record Office
NUHL        Nottingham University Hallward Library
NUMD        Nottingham University Manuscripts Department
MLSL         Mansfield Local Studies Library

# ILLUSTRATIONS (Including tables & Maps)

# NOTES

While every attempt has been made to give the correct spellings of peoples' names, they have been found to vary in different documents and newspaper reports. Anything that could not be read clearly will have been underlined. Where oral history has been used, it has to be accepted these are peoples memories, however in most cases the same story will have been heard from various people.

Attempts have been made to contact copyright owners where appropriate. If any have been inadvertently missed out this will be rectified in future editions.

# ACKNOWLEDGEMENTS

Many people have shown an interest in the work for my original MA dissertation [Nottingham 1997] and subsequently this book, for which I am grateful. While it is not possible to name everyone individually I would like to mention the following, some who sadly are no longer with us but still deserve acknowledgement:-

Librarians at Mansfield, (especially David Crute), Forest Town, Nottingham, Salisbury, Stamford, Ripon, Northallerton, Rhyl, Godalming, Guildford, Grantham.

Archivists at Nottingham Archive Office, Hallward Library Nottingham University, (especially the staff in Manuscripts Department of the East Midland Section), The National Archives (formerly Public Record Office), Kew, and Flintshire Record Office.

The Curator and Staff of Mansfield Museum and Art Gallery with special acknowledgement to Liz Weston and Jodie Henshaw. Peter Simkins, Historian, Imperial War Museum. The Curator of The Royal Engineers Museum, Chatham. Nicholas Nightingale and Rose Horscroft, Y.M.C.A. London. Jeoffrey Palmer, Y.M.C.A. Historian, London. Members of the Salvation Army Mansfield.

Steve Bray, Warden, Sherwood Pines Forest, Clipstone.

Mr & Mrs J Newton, Mrs Brown, Mrs Storey, Rhoda Cope, Kenneth Green, Eric Beadsmoore, Audrey Mills, Richard Wilkinson, Glyn Marples, and others who have contributed with oral history.

Rhoda Cope, Jeoff Fareham, Tim Priestly for information from postcard collections. Ben Houfton for use of Houfton photograph, Caroline Chaloner for use of Chesshire [sic] letters. Robert & Ann Hood for access to artefacts. Alan Clarke, Mr & Mrs Winter, John Danbury and numerous other people for documents, photographs, diaries, autograph books, letters etc.

Professor John Beckett & Doctor David Marcombe for past help and encouragement, [their words remain with me].

Shlomo & Lorraine Dowen of Forest Town Heritage Group for support and encouragement.

My friend Carole Lemmon for proof reading the first draft and my friend Shirley Blythe for the final proof read, my son Glyn for his help with internet research and purchasing post cards, my nephew D. Middlemiss, (formerly WFR Tidworth) for help and information, Tim Priestly for advice and encouragement. My daughter Carol and Glyn's partner Liz for encouragement, and husband Malcolm for support and help with layout, maps and the index.

To anyone whose name has inadvertently been forgotten, my apologies, everyone's help and encouragement has been valued and appreciated.

# PREFACE

This book looks at a period in history that was a poignant part of our history - this was the first World War 1914 -18, a war that altered the lives of many people as it extended from the anticipated few months into four years. The demand for an increased army meant the migration of young men from village, town and city. The men were encouraged to fight patriotically for their country, while industry and commercial enterprises were left to cope without them.

In the Nottinghamshire town of Mansfield the call for recruitment had a two-fold effect. A large number of men enlisted and moved away and an even greater number of soldiers moved into the area to live and train at Clipstone Camp. The hutted camp was just one of the camps especially erected to accommodate men of the new armies raised by Lord Kitchener. The building of such a camp had a big impact over all the area. The environment was affected. Concerns to health became an issue and increased expenditure was incurred by the local councils.

The camp and the integration of soldiers into the area brought additional spending power into the locality and quick thinking entrepreneurs took advantage of this. The social implications of the camp were many. Local people and organisations became involved in the moral welfare of the soldiers. Alternatively the moral welfare of young girls was a concern and prostitutes were banned from the vicinity of the camp.

Additionally the war affected production in the industries of Mansfield, work stopped on the sinking of Clipstone Colliery and the completion of the Mansfield Railway was delayed. Beds in the hospitals were needed for war wounded. Schools and local women became involved in events to raise funds and equipment for those participating in the war. However, for the communities of Mansfield, the camp played a significant part in the people's war.

********

The book is written so that each chapter has its own individual history as part of the bigger picture.

# 1 - INTRODUCTION - 1914

In the summer of 1914 the mood of the population was unsettled as the probability of war was rumoured. Tuesday 4th August 1914 should have been the day British people returned to work after the annual Bank Holiday, instead, the government extended the holiday until the Thursday. This was part of a series of emergency measures to counteract the temperament and spending of the nation. It was just the beginning. Many changes and decisions would affect the population over the next four years. The ultimate decision to go to war is one that will never be forgotten. It changed the lives of the British people forever. At 10.30pm on Tuesday 4th August 1914, a Privy Council was held at Buckingham Palace. Only the King, one minister and two court officials were present. This small council sanctioned, 'the proclamation of a state of war with Germany from 11pm'.[1] In reality, the holiday for the British people was over. The country was at war.

The Prime Minister's diary for the 4th August 1914 recorded 'the House took the fresh news today very calmly and with a good deal of dignity'.[2] The government did not predict a long disruptive war, and their preparations were limited. Lord Haldane's reforms to the army were credited with a British Expeditionary Force being established and ready to send overseas. An army that it is argued was "the best trained, best organised and best equipped British Army that ever went forth to war".[3] It was, however, an army that was deficient in the equipment required for siege and trench warfare, elements that were to prove essential in this war.[4] The Navy was ready and waiting. Instructions to "Commence hostilities with Germany"[5] were dispatched by Winston Churchill. The decision to go to war was confirmed. No consideration had been given to the country's industrial resources, or a survey of manpower. No importance had been placed on a possible disruption to civilian life. It was anticipated that the war would be over by Christmas. The conflict would all occur at a distance, and it was considered that the civilian population would carry on as normal.

However, the first indications of disruption to normality had already started before the ultimate decision to go to war was declared. Correspondence on the 31st July 1914 from Colonel Willoughby at Welbeck Abbey (Notts.) to H. D. Argles at Thoresby Park, (Notts.) would be typical of others communicated throughout the country. The short but meaningful letter stated;

'I have received instructions that horse purchasing operations
may become necessary at any moment now'.

Within days, horses were being purchased locally and sent to the military depot at Aldershot, and the Yeomanry at Mansfield.[6]

*Extract from a Daily Account dated August 6th 1914*
## Purchase of Horses on Mobilization

| Name of Owners from whom Horses or Vehicles were purchased | | No | Price |
|---|---|---|---|
| Mr Kirkby | Southwell | 8 | £360 |
| W. Brown | Butcher - Southwell | 1 | £40 |
| Mr Lewin | Halam | 1 | £38 |
| Mr Brocklebank | Upton | 1 | £52 |
| W. N. Hickling Esq,. | Southwell | 1 | £35 |
| Mr Foster | Upton | 1 | £30 |
| Mr James | Bleasby, Notts. | 1 | £47 |
| Mr Carding | Combs Farm, Southwell | 1 | £37 |

The type of horse is also given i.e. 'Light Draught' or 'Riding'
Also if the purchase is subsidised or not subsidised

**Information from NUMD Ma2C 148/18/102**

In London, there was an awareness of the unrest within the empire. From 1st August 1914 a small number of enthusiastic men had enlisted at one of the Principle Recruiting Offices. On the morning of the 4th August 1914, the recruiting officer arrived to find a mass of volunteers waiting to enlist. This enlightened him as to the initial impact of the war.

Within days, patriotic fever had taken a hold and men were thronging to enlist causing immediate problems for unprepared authorities throughout the country. The government, equally unprepared, hurriedly invited Lord Kitchener to take over the War Office. He reluctantly accepted, and within a short space of time, he became a symbol of patriotism. At the first meeting of the war council on 5th August 1914, Kitchener expressed the opinion that the war would extend far beyond the few months predicted. He took immediate steps to increase the army, a procedure that was to have far reaching effects for the British people, and the local communities in which they lived.

Newspapers of the 7th August 1914 carried Kitchener's appeal to the people: 'Your King and Country Needs You'. The call for 100,000 men made readers aware of the national emergency and the need to increase the army. In reality Parliament had the previous day, authorised an increase in the army of 500,000 men. Such a vast increase only emphasised that despite Haldane's reforms of the British Army,[7] Britain was unprepared to enter the war. There was an urgency and a dependency placed on the young male population, some of whom had never had the right to vote in the public elections.[8] Young men aged between 19 and 30 were urged to give up at least three years of their lives (if not their life) for the safety of the Empire. Such was the initial appeal from Lord Kitchener to the population. These were young men on whom many industries and families were dependent, men who came under many pressures to react to Kitchener's request. This was just the beginning, as the fighting and the progression of the war expanded so too did the demand on the male population. Enlistment became compulsory, patriotism became obligatory, for the majority it was no longer a free choice.

As the armies of Great Britain swelled with the new recruits, existing military compounds quickly became exhausted. The demand for new accommodation became an urgent requirement. Where possible, established encampments were expanded or completely new military camps were erected. Large country estates became home to rows of canvas tents and uniformed personnel.

Illustration of a canvas [tents] camp.

The land, if not freely given, could be acquired under the Defence of the Realm Act. Such demands on the property of local gentry varied from the billeting of horses to accommodating tented camps or hutted encampments for soldiers.

The Nottinghamshire estates of Wollaton, Thoresby, and Welbeck had tented encampments on their land at various times during the war. Camps that could be erected and removed at short notice. They were less disruptive than the building of more permanent hutted camps.

Around October 1914 Canadian Remounts (horses) were being brought into the country where initially they were kept in Remount Depots under observation for a month. The horses were then billeted out to various country establishments where they had to be suitably fed and exercised until they were of a standard required by the army. Some came to North Nottinghamshire. Finding accommodation for them was organised by H.D. Argles the agent of Thoresby Park (Notts). He sent out a circular to relevant people saying that the Government would pay 20/- a week for looking after the remount horses. Offers of help came from local farms and even the Bolsover Colliery Company.[9] Horses soon began arriving and the distribution started.

## TELEGRAM
Received from Ollerton Post Office 11 November 1914
Handed in at OHMS Ormskirk at 10.40am received 11.15am

To Argles Thoresby Park Ollerton

25 Horses consigned Edwinstowe
20 Worksop left Ormskirk 10.15 am
and Seven Southwell 9.10 am.

Remounts Ormskirk

Information from NUMD Ma 2c 148/18/184

Additional to the need of horses, the expansion and creation of military establishments within the town and countryside was essential to the army. However, these created an added impact of the war on the civilian authorities, and many other establishments within society. The public was also greatly affected. In addition to the tented camps erected throughout the country, Nottinghamshire was chosen for one of the large hutted encampments that were to be built for the expanding army. The site selected was at Clipstone, in close proximity to the market town of Mansfield.

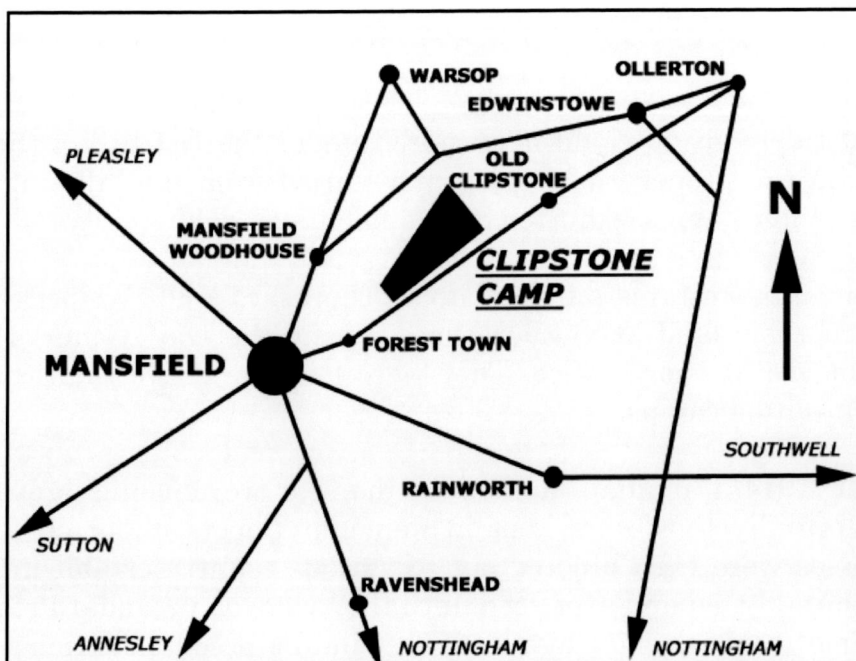

At the onset of war the town had a population of over 40,000 and was described as a 'busy and thriving town'.[10] It had many established industries such as textiles, iron foundries and tin box manufacturers. The chief industry of the area was coal mining. The opening out of the coalfields in close vicinity to Mansfield was both instrumental to the growth of the town and the development of new communities. Over 43 per cent of the local male population were employed in the coal mining industry. It was an industry that bred strong young men of the right calibre to be soldiers and they were encouraged to enlist.

Clipstone Camp - early photograph

The founding of the military camp near Mansfield had a significant effect on the local population. It resulted in thousands of men, (also women), migrating in and out of the area on a regular basis during the period of the war. The soldiers were not confined to camp boundaries, they encroached on the surrounding locality and became part of the people's war. Additionally the welfare of the soldiers was reliant on the voluntary work of the public, much of which took place within the camp perimeter. Historian J.P.Taylor maintains, that life changed with the impact of the Great War and 'The mass of the people became for the first time, active citizens'.[11] Nearly 100 years later active citizenship is still being encouraged by Britain's population.

The history of the Great War is recorded in many different ways. Political papers, regimental and oral histories, war diaries, war poems, and now the internet are all revealing in their information. Bloody battles of the war and life on the home front are well documented. Local histories written about the Great War are in a minority yet they are equally worthy of recording.

Mansfield, along with other areas in Britain was greatly affected by the impact of the war. The effect became more significant when a large military camp, Clipstone Camp, was established within a few miles of the town changing the landscape and peoples lives in a way previously unimagined.

# END NOTES

1    J P Taylor, *English History 1914-1918,* (Oxford 1965) p 2

2    As quoted in J Watson, *Success in British History Since 1914,* (1983) p. 11

3    As quoted in J P Taylor, *English History,* p. 8

4    J P Taylor, *English History,* p. 8

5    J M Bourne, *Britain and the Great War 1914-1918,* (1918) p. 8

6    NUMD Ma 2c 148/18/316 letter from Col C.H.Willoughby, Welbeck Abbey to H D Argles, Thoresby Park.

7    Haldane's Reforms were a series of far-ranging reforms of the British Army made from 1906 to 1912, named after Richard Burdon Haldane the Secretary of State for War.

8    Votes for all men over 21 -1918, aged 18 in 1969

9    NUMD Ma 2c 148/18/45

10    *The Railway News* 21/6/1913 as found in TNA: PRO RAIL 226/558

11    J P Taylor *English History,* p. 2

# 2 - RECRUITMENT

At the onset of the Great War the Nottinghamshire coalfield was about to be extended to the west of Mansfield and a new railway was in progress. Mansfield and the surrounding parishes had been expanding over the past two decades. The population had risen with the sinking of the new pits, and whole new communities had developed as miners and their families migrated into the area. At the declaration of war, the Mansfield population along with the rest of Britain, was asked to respond to the needs of the country. The poster declaring 'Your Country Needs You' was aimed at encouraging young men to enlist and fight for King and Country. However, this statement placed responsibility on the community as a whole, not just the young male population.

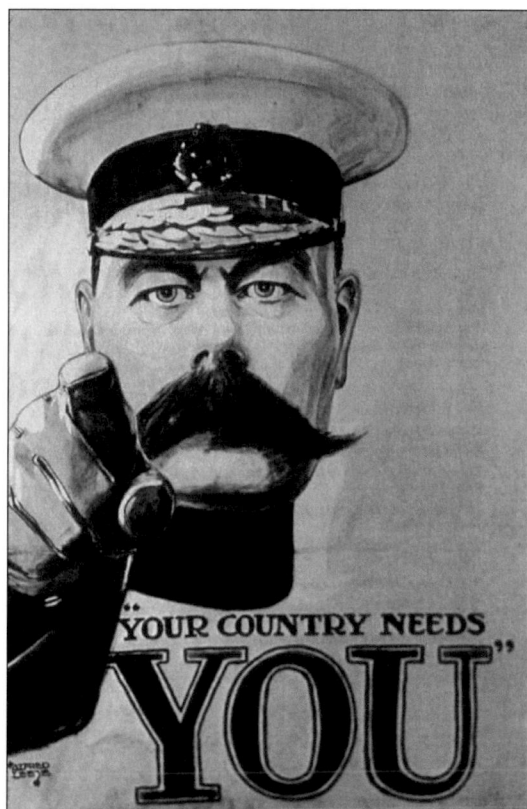

Mansfield is not a town noted for its military history or fortifications and in 1914 only a series of Drill Halls housed the military establishments of the town. There was the Drill Hall in Dame Flogan Street for a platoon of the Notts. Sherwood Yeomanry. Another Drill Hall for the Army was in West Gate, while the Mansfield Boys' Brigade and Cadet Company for young men over 17 used a Drill Hall on Bath Lane. Rural areas also had Boys' Brigade Companies in villages such as Pleasley and Forest Town.[1]

Within these establishments young men and boys were introduced to a military regime of discipline and drill, for some it would soon become a harsh reality.

The War Diary for Mansfield states:

> *'August 4th, Great sensation caused in Mansfield by the news of the declaration of war against Germany by Great Britain'.*[2]

One wonders how the writer established this reaction for the local newspapers do not portray any feeling of crowds massing in the market square in excited agitation, unlike the events in Trafalgar Square, London. The Mansfield local newspapers of that period could not be accused of over re-action to the news of war. They were published within days of war being declared, yet the short articles contained within the middle pages, did very little to alert readers to the events of the previous days.

Despite the lack of journalistic impact it soon became evident that sections of the local community were immediately responding to the news. Red Cross detachments were busy with extra training, ladies were showing a willingness to serve as nurses. Twelve men from the Mansfield St John's Ambulance Brigade responded to a War Office call to join the expeditionary force. The Territorial Army assembled and left Mansfield for Newark creating an air of excitement in the town.

Men of the Mansfield Territorial Battalion were amongst the first men to face the patriotic challenge. They returned from a camp at Hunmanby, (Yorks.) on Monday 3rd August 1914, and the following evening 'they were summoned to take part in the defence of their country.'[3] Territorial Buglers circulated the area and called the men to attend the Drill Hall where their kit was ready and waiting. Crowds of people were in the town to witness their departure by train to Newark.

It was the first time in the Battalion's history that Mansfield had seen the Territorials with their full equipment. Excitement would have overruled any sense of fear that either the soldiers or their families may have had. The scene was one of festivity, and the people of the town could be forgiven if they did not grasp the full seriousness of the occasion.

No indication is given of how many men left the town in what appeared to be the first of many similar military departures. The large numbers of soldiers had obviously far more impact than the departure of sailors at the station two days earlier. The Mansfield Reporter Newspaper admitted to its readers:-

*'It almost omitted to make mention of the scenes witnessed at the railway station on Monday, when sailors were seen leaving for their headquarters.*
*Some very affectionate leave-takings were seen, but as the trains moved away there was generally a cheer to lighten the hearts of those who were answering their country's call.'[4]*

Throughout the country similar scenes and departures were taking place. Leave-takings from the heavily populated areas of towns and cities with railway stations would witness different departures to those occurring in outlying villages. Departures from the rural areas had less impact but were equally significant to the individuals concerned. When the decision to raise a second army was made, pressure was generated from the government down to each individual community. Each community was prone to different pressures because of its location, industries, and the influence of local aristocrats and employers.

Welbeck Abbey circa 1913

One of the most influential landowners in Nottinghamshire was the Duke of Portland of Welbeck Abbey, eight miles from Mansfield. The Duke's participation in recruiting campaigns and other war-related events in the counties of Nottinghamshire and Derbyshire were consistent with his reputation. An added inducement, had one been needed, was his association with Lord Kitchener who was often a guest at Welbeck.

Ten days after the declaration of war, Kitchener, Admiral Prince Louis of Battenberg, and other guests dined with the Duke of Portland in London. Kitchener was asked for his predications about the war, he stated that it would last four years, also that the size of the army would increase each year.[5]

The growth of the army was initially dependent on enthusiastic volunteers, who were encouraged and praised from every quarter. An emphasis was placed on fighting not just for King and Country, but for the town, work place and even a soldier's family.

Volunteers Mansfield Colliery St John's Ambulance Brigade. European War 1918

It was something of which everyone could be proud. Death and the horror of the war came secondary to the cause. Those who declined the opportunity of glory were shunned by society. White feathers signified cowardice and were given to those deemed as such. Advertisements in newspapers were aimed at the men who had so far declined to enlist.

NOW THEN, **YOU.**

ENLIST NOW
100,0[00] [M]EN
WA[NTE]D.

Look here, my lad, if you're old enough to walk out with my daughter, you are
old enough to fight for her and your Country.
At any Post Office you can obtain the address of the nearest Recruiting Office.

From Mansfield & Sutton Reporter 29 January 1915

Equally the advertisements reflected on wives, children, families and sweethearts of such men; did they want this kind of person in their lives? Families had to face their neighbours; men had to face their work colleagues and their employers. Pressure was everywhere.

Responsibility towards recruitment was placed initially on the Lords-Lieutenants of the counties. A War Office circular signed by Kitchener stated:-

*'Sir, In the present grave emergency, the War Office looks with the utmost confidence to you for a continuance of the invaluable help which you have given in the past. I therefore desire to invite your co-operation in the work of raising additional numbers of regular troops required at once for the army.*[6]

The letter requested the Lords-Lieutenants used their influence in recruiting 100,000 men needed for a second army. Accommodation for the men was to be near existing regular depots and counties would not be responsible for the clothing and equipping of the enthusiastic volunteers.[7] An immediate reaction to the letter in Nottinghamshire was for it to be published in the local newspapers. The Mansfield Reporter on 14th August 1914 also printed a request for civilian recruits for the regular army. They would enlist initially for one year as opposed to the three years of military conscripts.[8]

This request for civilian recruits was more specific in detail. The trades and specialist skills required were for the administration and operation of the enlarged military regime:- Clerks, hospital and veterinary staff, blacksmiths, boilermakers, bakers, butchers, store-men. The list of men required was vast, and the man's trade determined his daily rate of pay.

Motor cyclists were required to take along their motorbike and accessories such as goggles, overalls and gauntlets.

The non-fighting personnel could enlist from a wider age group than the 18 to 35 year old recruits required for Kitchener's Second Army. The minimum age was 20 and the upper limit 55 for retired army artificers.[9]

Opportunity abounded for public-spirited citizens who wanted to do their bit towards winning the war. How well the people in and around Mansfield responded to this appeal is unknown, for irrespective of how essential the civilian recruits were to the war effort, they did not receive the same acclaim as the fighting men.

A Recruiting Office was opened in Mansfield Town Hall and by the end of August 300 men had joined the colours. The majority of these recruits were from the mining industry and the 'Mansfield Reporter' was quick to alert the public of this. Captain Jeoffcock the Recruiting Officer was hopeful that men from other trades and occupations would also show their enthusiasm to fight for King and Country.[10]

Mansfield Town Hall & Market Square

Men from areas outside the town were equally encouraged to enlist at the Mansfield Office. For some, Kitchener's poster, along with a few drinks was the spur! One young man who worked at Welbeck Colliery told of how he went into Mansfield with his mates. The war had been on about a fortnight and they had been in the pub in the market square for a drink. On leaving the pub to go home and get ready for work on the afternoon shift they saw Kitchener's photo on the poster outside the Town Hall.

One of them said "*how about joining up?*" They dared each other and went in! It was only later when reality struck home.[11]

Additionally the Duke of Portland urged all men to come forward and join the colours. An extra emphasis was placed on the importance of Nottinghamshire not falling behind other counties in recruitment. Furthermore, the Duke of Portland hoped Nottinghamshire would lead the way.[12] 'The prestige of the county was a significant element of the war'.

John P. Houfton was another person who played a notable part in many of the local recruiting campaigns.[13] He was well known and respected in the local coal industries, and had been instrumental in establishing coal mines and colliery villages for the Bolsover Colliery Company.[14] At the outbreak of war, John P. Houfton lived near Mansfield in close proximity to the Mansfield Colliery and its associated village of Forest Town. During the second week of September 1914, great scenes prevailed in this small village where the focus of the excitement was the Drill Hall.

Drill Hall, Forest Town

At short notice, a meeting was called, and the colliery band paraded round the streets signalling the importance of the occasion. Military personnel, colliery managers and local dignitaries joined John P. Houfton to speak to the assembled audience. The urgency of recruiting for King and Country was stressed, and the emphasis was placed on joining the County Battalion of the Sherwood Foresters.[15]

The 8th Battalion Sherwood Foresters, based at Newark were part of the North Midland Division who, as a complete unit, had been accepted for the field army abroad. The assembled crowd was told this was a great honour. An honour that was in danger of becoming a disgrace to the county as the 8th Battalion was urgently in need of men. Of the men who had previously been sent, some had returned to Newark as they were undersized or physically unfit. Now eighty more recruits were required by the end of the week. The assembly was asked, "could they not get that number from Forest Town?" [16]

Many aspects of the war were fed to the people gathered in the Drill Hall. They heard how Germany had started the war, how Britain was keeping its word to Belgium and of the cost and self-sacrifice by everyone as heroic young men enlisted and left their homes. John P. Houfton spoke of four meetings in Derbyshire he had attended the previous week. At those meetings a total of 750 men had been recruited, 'the bulk of whom were miners, men of whom the country might be proud.'[17] An occupation he stressed "rendered them not only intelligent but made their muscles hard and rendered them fit for licking into shape to join the army abroad."[18] The power of words was used to stir up the self-esteem of each miner present. The prestige of the Mansfield Colliery, and of the people of Forest Town was stressed.

Mansfield Colliery

The gathering were reminded that because of the recent visit by the King and Queen,[19] Forest Town was known all over England. Miners from the village worked at Mansfield Colliery, and 168 men from the colliery had already enlisted. Behind they had left their wives and children. John P. Houfton said the Colliery Company would look after the men's dependants.[20] Cheering accompanied the speeches and patriotic songs were sung with accompaniment from the band. All of this added to the pressure placed on the young men who, as they moved forward to give their name received loud acclaim. Many accolades were placed on young shoulders as they enlisted that day.

Forest Town Recruits Marching to Mansfield Station
Postcard produced by G. S. Ellis Photographer, Mansfield

Public meetings such as this were a common occurrence in Mansfield and the surrounding villages during the early years of the war. Always there was a spur to entice the men away from safe employment and the security of their families. Incentives were given by those who were not immune to the effects of war. They watched their sons and employees go off to war, many who would not return.[21] Grief was often secondary to patriotic duty, and for the leading figures of the locality, their obligation was to encourage and publicise the requirements of the country.

Publicity through posters, the newspapers and the spoken word at public meetings or on the factory floor, were all essential elements of the recruiting campaign.

Mansfield newspapers in common with others all over the country placed a great importance on photographs of men who had enlisted. Short but descriptive captions informed readers of the regiment joined, home address and place of employment before enlistment. Added captions such as 'Sons of', 'Nephews of' 'Brothers join the Army' gave added prestige to both family and neighbourhood. In doing so, an attempt was made to embarrass those men or families still not committed. Additionally letters and poems condoning able-bodied-men who were still at home, were printed in the newspapers. Men, who until conscription was brought in, could remain unknown.

## AN APPEAL TO THE SLACKER
### (Or A CALL TO ARMS).

To You who watch and stand and gaze.

As in a trance or in a maze,

Who are not moved by country's call,

But stand aloof and see it fall;

If you but live, you will repent,

You sluggards! Oh, you indolent!

To you, you chicken-hearted chaps,

Who stay at home on mothers' laps,

When other mothers' nobler sons.

Go forth to meet and fight the Huns.

*Extract from a poem in The Mansfield Reporter and Sutton Times*
*25th September 1914 written by F S Warsop.*

The necessity to increase the armies became urgent as the death toll mounted and insufficient men volunteered. To rectify the situation the government introduced conscription in January 1916. Applications for exemption were made. Tribunal Courts were established throughout the country to hear applications from those who believed they had genuine reasons not to enlist, and from those who chose not to. In Mansfield, the applicants appeared before many public figures that were prominent leaders of the voluntary recruiting campaigns. They now had to be impartial at the tribunal hearings. These became a regular feature in local newspapers disclosing the name of the objector, attempted justification and conclusion.

**MANSFIELD TRIBUNAL**

Lengthy Sittings
on Tuesday and Last Night

*Mansfield Chronicle 2 March 1916*

**TRIBUNAL**
**MANSFIELD MILITARY**
Postponement for many
married men
*Mansfield Chronicle 13 July 1916*

Men appealed stating their widowed mothers, children, sick and crippled relatives were dependent on them. Some were given exemption, others were refused.

One such Tribunal at the end of May 1916 heard requests from a Platelayer, Miner, Road Mender, Young Farmer and an Ammunition Box Maker, all were refused exemption. [22]

Some employers applied fearing for their business and livelihood if they or their employees enlisted. Undertaker and Monumental Mason, Jesse Alan Head who applied for absolute exemption. He stated: -

*"three out of four of his men had joined the colours, and if he himself was called up he would have no one to put in charge of the undertaking business. He furnished three or four funerals per week and he himself made as many as seven or eight coffins in a week...additionally he did motor carting work taking provisions etc to the camp."*[23]

His case was deferred until October 31st. Requests by some caused a smile at the tribunals:-

*Arthur Boole of Hermitage Lane appealed for his son, Walter Boole, a horseman whose duties were to cart coal and firewood. He was asked "Do you think that carting coal is indispensable to the interests of the country?" Old Mr Boole replied "You cannot burn coal without wood, eh?"*

The application was refused.[24] So too was the request from a pianoforte tuner and dealer who considered it was in the national interests that pianos should be tuned regularly in the war.[25]

While some applicants received a temporary reprieve from enlistment, others found occupation and families were secondary to the cause. The newspaper headline, 'Indispensables Not Exempted'[26] signified that town and community had to survive without them.

Conscientious Objectors [people who refused to enlist, fight and kill] such as Ernest Smith of Murray Street Mansfield were sometimes given the opportunity to find alternative war work.[27]

Throughout the county, a public-spirited attitude was apparent from the onset of the war. Names of personnel enlisting were noted in minute books, and school magazines etc. Mr Jagger headmaster told a local newspaper, "the response of the Old Boy's of Queen Elizabeth's Grammar School to the country's call has been splendid." And he proudly listed over 100 name of former pupils.

Religious establishments also honoured their members who had chosen to enlist. Guardians of the Mansfield Workhouse did not extend their praises to a Roll of Honour, nevertheless they were pleased to report the decline in the numbers of tramps seeking hospitality. A decline they attributed to patriotic enlistment![28]

Rolls of Honour [men enlisting] became a regular feature in the local newspapers as employers from all types of industry advertised the loyal attitude of their workforce.

## Mansfield's Loyalty
### As listed in Mansfield Reporter
### 29th January 1915

| Industries | Number Serving | Percentage of Eligible |
|---|---|---|
| Mansfield Corporation | | |
|     Borough Surveyors Dept. | 9 | 12 |
|     Gas Dept. | 11 | 25 |
| Post Office | 20 | - |
| Mansfield Engineering Co. | 12 | 50 |
| Sherwood Foundry | 9 | 25 |
| Meadow Foundry | 20 | 90 |
| Union Foundry | 35 | - |
| Sanderson & Robinson's Foundry | 15 | - |
| M G & A Bradley Ltd | 6 | 100 |
| Harwood Cash & Co. | 6 | 50 |
| Reed Mill | 15 | 25 |
| Hermitage Mill | 16 | 70 |
| Alcock & Co. (Factory) | 3 | 40 |
| Mansfield Tramways | 28 | 60 |
| Mansfield Shoe Co. | 9 | 25 |
| Mansfield Co-operative Society | 12 | 13 |
| W Hollins & Co. (Pleasley) | 25 | 13 |

Additionally over 800 miners from local collieries had enlisted. The small numbers enlisted from commercial and manufacturing firms are explained by several of the mills employing a large percentage of female labour, or men occupied on Government work.

While employers took pride in their employees who had recruited, they were at the same time faced with the consequences of a loss of manpower. The coal mining industry who had encouraged thousands of young men to enlist, suffered a decline in output.[29] The completion of the Mansfield Railway was delayed and this was attributed to a lack of manpower and equipment. Local agriculture relied on temporary military labour. Hubert Argles, the Agent for the Thoresby Estate liased between tenant farmers and military personnel for this purpose.[30]

For example, when Mr J H Driffill, Farleys Farm, Tuxford wrote in September 1915 for help with the harvest he was told:

> 'Major Worthington, Yeomanry Camp, No 6 Lines Clipstone Camp, Nr Mansfield is supplying these soldiers by order from General Sir James Trotter. If the soldiers can be sent to you, Major Worthington will wish you to send a conveyance for them to Clipstone.'

The use of female labour for agriculture was not evident in the locality.

Mansfield Brewery despite reduced opening hours incurred by the Defence of the Realm Act, found trade increased but they had to cope with fewer employees as many were in the armed forces.[31]

The war affected local councils in many ways and recruitment was one of them. Mansfield Woodhouse Council received memorandums from the Local Government Board. These suggested employees who were in the Territorials or Army Reserve should be given leave of absence and replaced by temporary substitutes.[32] The Road Foreman and other employees were recorded as leaving in this way. In November 1915, the Sanitary Inspector Mr E Parker was given permission to join the Forces, unlike the Medical Officer of Health who in February 1916 it was said could not be spared. Payments to dependant relatives of Mansfield Council employees who had joined the colours were discussed,[33] along with additional premises required for recruiting purposes. It appears that the Mayor's Parlour and Card Room were already being used[34] and more rooms in the Town Hall were agreed on after discussions with the Recruiting Officer,[35] and lease agreements agreed with the War Office.[36] The Mayor authorised the Town Clerk to obtain posters while he proposed a public meeting to encourage recruiting.[37]

The progression of the war created many new issues for discussion such as the setting up of tribunals for starred and indispensable men in November 1915,[38] and National Service.[39] The release of The Borough Surveyor and Medical Officer of Health created problems, and the decision to advertise the latter post to 'suitably qualified ladies' was taken.[40] The health of the local people was an important consideration.

The Annual Report of the Sanitary Inspector for the year 1914 stated there were no troops in the Borough during that year. However, the anticipated building of a large military camp on the outskirts of the town did give cause for anxiety, because of the spreading of infectious diseases.[41] For the local councils and the whole locality, the camp highlighted another aspect of recruitment. The community, which was still adjusting to its own response to war and the recruitment of local men now found itself giving hospitality to thousands of soldiers. For the communities of Mansfield the establishing of the camp gave a new dimension to the war.

# END NOTES

1   Linneys Almanac              1914
2   Linneys Almanac              1916
3   Mansfield Reporter      7 Aug.1914  p. 5 col. 4
4       ibid.               7 Aug.1914  p. 5 col. 5
5   Portland Duke of,*Men Women & Things,* (1937) p 207
6   Mansfield Reporter      14 Aug.1914  p. 3 col. 2
7       ibid.               14 Aug.1914  p. 3 col. 8
8       ibid.               14 Aug.1914  p. 8 col. 3
9       ibid.               28 Aug.1914  p. 8 col. 2
10      ibid.               28 Aug.1914  p. 8 col. 2
11  Oral History tape in private collection
12  Mansfield Reporter      28 Aug.1914  p. 8 col. 2
13  John P. Houfton, appointed Manager and Secretary of Bolsover Colliery Company January 1980, General Manager 1890, Director 1910. retained a seat on the Board until his death in November 1920.
14  Bolsover 1891, Creswell 1896, Mansfield,1905, Rufford 1913. The sinking of Clipstone was halted when war broke out, it resumed in 1920.
15  Mansfield Reporter      11 Sep.1914  p. 9 col. 1-3
16      ibid.               11 Sep.1914  p. 9 col. 1-3
17      ibid.               11 Sep.1914  p. 9 col. 1-3
18      ibid.               11 Sep.1914  p. 9 col. 1-3
19  The King and Queen touring Nottinghamshire in June 1914 visited Forest Town, where at their request they entered a coal miner's house and chatted to the occupants.
20  Mansfield Reporter      11 Sep.1914  p. 9 col. 1-3
21  The Duke of Portland's son Titchfield served in the Household Cavalry. John P. Houfton's son Charles, served in the Sherwood Foresters he was killed Nov.1915.
22  Mansfield Chronicle     1 Jun. 1916 p.1
23      ibid.               13 Jul. 1916 p.1
24      ibid.               2 Mar. 1916 p.2
25      ibid.               2 Mar. 1916 p.2
26      ibid.               2 Mar. 1916 p.2 col. 1
27      ibid.               13 Jul. 1916
28      ibid.               7 May 1915 p. 3 col. 7
29  Griffin A.R. *Mining in the East Midlands 1550-1947,* (1971) p 171
30  NUMD Ma 2c 148/19/1-420
31  Philip Bristow, *The Mansfield Brew,* (Ringwood Hants 1976) p 77
32  NA DC/MW/1/3/4/6        10 Aug.1914
33  NA DC/M 1/1/2/23        4 Sep.1914
34      ibid.               7 Feb.1916
35      ibid.               7 Feb.1916
36  NA DC/M 1/1/2/24        6 Mar.1916
37  NA DC/M 1/1/2/23        7 Dec.1914
38      ibid.               5 Nov.1915
39      ibid.               27 Mar.1917
40      ibid.               27 Mar.1917
41      ibid.               31 Dec.1914

Fighting for King and Country

A post card showing the position of Clipstone Camp.
This was available for soldiers to purchase and send to family and
friends.

# 3 - CLIPSTONE CAMP

During the First World War a large military camp was established near Mansfield in Nottinghamshire to accommodate and train thousands of soldiers. It was located in open countryside, heath land known to some as the Ling Forest,[1] and situated between the new mining village of Forest Town and the tiny hamlet of Clipstone.[2] This was an area more acquainted with the partridge shooting of the Duke of Portland and his sporting colleagues, or the pilfering by professional poachers.[3]

Disruptions had recently occurred in the vicinity when the Bolsover Colliery Company had commenced the boring of the Clipstone Colliery. This project had to stop with the commencement of war and did not restart until 1920. Near to the site of the colliery, the company had planned to build 700 houses between Clipstone and Forest Town. The Duke of Portland had given a wood to the Bolsover Colliery Company suitable for recreational purposes, which was in close proximity to the site of the proposed new houses. The Duke, forever heedful of the needs of the mining communities, was soon to see a different emphasis placed on the land when the wooden huts of the large military camp replaced the anticipated mining village. The camp predicted to house upwards of 25,000 soldiers was constructed alongside the road to Mansfield[4] and was known as Clipstone Camp.

It is unknown if the Duke of Portland owned the land where the camp was built, or if the Bolsover Colliery Company had already bought or leased it from him,[5] however a large proportion of the countryside that was used for military training did belong to the Duke. The decision to site a camp at Clipstone was made in the autumn of 1914 when the War Office found it necessary to expand the 'hutting' programme yet again. Other new sites chosen at that time were 'Larkhill, Perham Down, Fovant near Salisbury, Whitley Common and Bramshott, near Aldershot, Kinmel Park in North Wales, Prees Heath and Oswestry, in Shropshire.'[6] Why the site at Clipstone, near Mansfield was selected is unknown.

Even before the onset of the war large country estates such as Thoresby Hall in Nottinghamshire were already being utilised as canvas camp sites for military personnel.

It is surmised that such estates were not suited to the vast hutted encampments need to cope with influx of recruits to Kitchener's new armies. The terrain and the isolation of Clipstone would, however, have made the area suitable for that purpose. It is reasonable to assume that the Duke of Portland or John P Houfton, General Manager of the Bolsover Colliery

Thoresby Hall

Company, would have raised no objections to the use of the land. Both of these men were ardent campaigners for the patriotic needs of the country.

Under the Defence of the Realm Act the War Office had 'the powers to take land or buildings or construct works' if the need arose.[7] They were anxious that the setting up the various camps and training grounds should disrupt civilian life as little as possible. Land owners and tenants property had to be respected. Among the many letters and directives issued were instructions to avoid damage to crops, tillage, and livestock. The care of parks and woodlands was emphasised and the digging of trenches must be of a temporary nature. The land should as soon as possible be reinstated to its previous condition.[8] This order obviously lost its priority as the war extended, and thousands of men migrated in and out of the area around Clipstone. Over seven hectares of land, trenches and rifle butts can still be found in the former heath-land training area. The land is now part of a vast pine forest.[9]

As Clipstone Camp was constructed in an area of open heath-land, forest, and agricultural land, public utilities such as water and sewerage were not yet extended to the area. The public highway from Ollerton to Mansfield, which ran at the side of the proposed camp was a dusty track occasionally used by horse drawn farm wagons, and pedestrians. On reaching the populated village of Forest Town, the road, despite being in greater use was still unmade. A War Office directive stated:

> 'Unnecessary damage to roads must be avoided in every possible way. Mechanical and other heavy transport should not make use of roads that are not properly bottomed unless absolutely necessary.'[10]

The Mansfield to Ollerton Road was used for the construction of the camp, and by the troops once the camp was in operation. The state of the road and the sanitary arrangements of the camp were regularly discussed at both Mansfield and the Mansfield Woodhouse Council meetings. Although the camp was built in the parish of Mansfield Woodhouse it still created many problems for the Mansfield Town Council.

On learning of the proposed camp in November 1914, Mansfield Woodhouse Council immediately wrote to the War Office in regard to the sanitation arrangements for the camp. The reply stated that careful consideration was being given to sanitation arrangements, and that they hoped to eleviate any possibility of pollution.[11] However, the concern of both Mansfield Woodhouse and Mansfield Council continued until the end of 1917. Repeated correspondence was entered into which resulted in meetings between the Council, the Military Authorities, and County Representatives.

The major concern was the disposal of sewage from the camp, and the possible contamination of the nearby Clipstone well which supplied water for domestic purposes. Periodic bacteriological samples of water from the well were extracted and tested. The results of a test in July 1917 alerted the Mansfield Council to discontinue using the well until a Chlorinating Plant was installed. An alternative water supply had to be taken from the well at Rainworth until pumping from Clipstone could recommence. The annual report of the Medical Officer for the year 1917 confirmed the main cause of contamination was attributed to the camp and the inadequate disposal of camp excreta.

It is difficult to assess which issue dominated the council meetings most, the sanitation problems at the camp, or the state of the access road to it. Work started on the construction of huts towards the end of November 1914. Early in December, complaints were sent to the War Office concerning 'the bad condition of the road as a result of the extraordinary traffic in connection with haulage of timber and materials for the new camp.'[12] The camp site was being approached from Mansfield and in an attempt to improve the situation the contractor was asked if an alternative route could be taken.[13] This was tried but was only succeeded in causing damage to a new area and affected the villages of Mansfield Woodhouse and Warsop.

**Picture showing the state of the road at Forest Town
en route from Mansfield to Clipstone Camp**

The cost of repairing the roads was of utmost concern. Mansfield Woodhouse council minutes record the Road Board had promised early repayment of the council expenditure.[14] The occupation of the camp from May 1915 only increased the damage to the road as thousands of marching feet, and horses hooves hammered the surface. Car wheels further added to the destruction as local entrepreneurs developed taxi services to the camp. The large increase in pedestrian and motor traffic to and from Mansfield and the Clipstone Camp added even further to the work and expenditure of the Mansfield Council.

Concern was also expressed that 'the general public especially the school children were in danger.'[15] And a scheme of road widening and consultation with property owners had to be undertaken in the town.

The damage to road surfaces and concern with sewage were only two of the local authorities concerns. The position of the camp meant that whatever service was required it incurred both negotiations and expenditure. Discussions between the War Office, various committees and banks to arrange loans, were all time consuming. Responsibility for the expenditure had to be agreed by all parties concerned. An indication of costs are given in the Annual Reports.

| COUNCIL EXPENDITURE RELATIVE TO CAMP | YEAR ENDING | |
|---|---|---|
| | 31 March 1916 | 31 March 1917 |
| Road Improvements | £1150 | £1500 |
| Extraordinary Traffic | £200 | £70 |
| Water Supply | £1497 | £2759 |
| Electricity Supply | £4144 | £2961 |
| TOTAL | £6991 | £7290 |

**Source N.A.O. DC/M 1/1/25 & DC/M 1/1/26**

Clipstone Camp was isolated. It needed a water supply. Added to this was the concern with water pollution. A request for a telephone line was made by the military authorities to the Mansfield Post Office Engineering Department. They in turn had to request the permission of the relevant Councils to erect and maintain a line between Forest Town and the camp.[16] The cost of installing a supply of electricity to the camp was estimated at £5,000. One mile of the mains was to be laid underground and the rest carried overhead. For this the consent of landowners was needed.[17] The installing of this electricity supply procured the first alternating current in Mansfield.[18] Clipstone Camp finally had an electricity supply by the end of July 1915.[19]

The hastily built camp caused greater disruption to the area than the sinking of the Mansfield (Crown Farm) Colliery and the construction of its associated village of Forest Town a decade earlier. In 1915 when Mansfield and the surrounding community were still coming to terms with the onset of war overseas, they suddenly found it was impacting on the locality in a way never envisaged.

The wider community also became aware of Clipstone and other camps when adverts appeared in newspapers such as in the Lichfield Mercury 26th March 1915 (see below).

**TENDERS**
**ARMY CONTRACTS**

Tenders for the Supply of Coal, Coke, Kindling Wood and Palliasse Straw at the following Hutment Camps:-

CLIPSTONE CAMP, near Mansfield
BROCTON CAMP, near Rugeley
PENKRIDGE BANK, near Rugeley
RICHMOND, Yorks

for the period from the opening of each camp to the 30th of June 1916, and also for the following services:- Washing, repairing and remaking Barrack and Hospital Bedding, etc., Removal of ashes and rubbish, will be received at the under mentioned office until 12 noon on Monday, the 5th April 1915.

Forms of tender can be obtained on application to the District Barrack Officer, Northern Command, York.
Headquarters, Northern Command, York.

Locally, on the 12th March 1915 the Mansfield Reporter newspaper declared 'a visit to the camp [Clipstone] was a revelation and the impression upon entering it, is that one is in a great wilderness of timber. On all sides men are carrying wood, or sawing and hammering it, skeletons of huts are seen everywhere.'[20]

When the first contingent of soldiers arrived at the camp they considered it 'depressing, the rough and unfinished condition of every visible object seemed to promise, not only present discomfort but a vast amount of future work.' In those early days the camp was considered 'The Land of Chaos.'[21]

The Nottingham Guardian also described the camp as 'scarcely an inspiring sight. The wooden rectangular structures which differ from each other only in a matter of size are painted an inconspicuous grey, great piles of timber, the toiling engines, uneven ground and the clang of hammers suggest some great industrial undertaking rather than the panoply of war. Even the lighting installation is not complete and candles are the chief form of illuminant.'[22]

The main contractor for the construction of the camp was W Hodson and Sons of Nottingham, and at least two firms in Mansfield were also involved, George Bradley & Sons, and Boalers. The building of the huge wooden complex provided well-paid employment for 400 men.

The work was carried out under the supervision of the director of barrack construction. The original date for completion was 6th February 1915, but this date was contingent on a satisfactory supply of material, which was not realised, and also on certain other technical considerations.[23]

**An early photo of the camp**

Additionally the Mansfield Reporter in March suggested that 12 battalions were to be accommodated at the camp, and the estimated size of the camp was:-

60 buildings to each battalion

The huts which would accommodate 30 men
were erected in avenues one mile in length.
Parts of the camp were half a mile wide.

There were additional huts for
cooking, washing, latrines, stables, and equipment storage.
There were spacious huts for
officers and sergeants of each battalion.[24]

This was an early estimate and as the war extended so did the camp. Plans, later discovered, reveal there was accommodation for twenty battalions.[25]

**Plan of Clipstone Camp circa 1918**

At the onset many facilities were of a temporary nature. The post was dealt with in a large marquee which at one time dealt with a record of 3,189 items posted in one day prior to the building of wooden YMCA huts with postal facilities.[26]

A temporary hospital was established by ladies from Surrey after they discovered there was no military hospital at the new camp when their own Brigade (The Royal Fusiliers) moved to Clipstone. A hut which had a large kitchen and rooms suitable for wards that would accommodate 60 patients was found. 'The necessary equipment from Woodcote Park was conveyed north in the ever ready ambulance wagon and local equipment was lent until the war office supplies arrived.'[27]

So unknown was the camp to start with that when at the beginning of May when an advance party of the University and Public Schools Brigade (UPS) was sent from Epsom to Clipstone, the report came back that they could not find it. They had been sent to Clipstone near Market Harborough, and it was thought to have been a practical joke. However a few days later, after telephone calls and correspondence, information was received that 'it was much regretted, but a clerical error had been made.' The first instruction should have read 'Clipstone, near Mansfield.'[28]

Five thousand men of the UPS Royal Fusiliers were the first troops posted to Clipstone. They had previously been stationed at Woodcote, Epsom, in comfortable quarters with garden plots. Their first impression of Clipstone earned it the name 'Land of Chaos'[29] They arrived at Edwinstowe on the 12th May 1915 and had to march four miles in the rain and were ankle deep in mud. The camp that greeted them was still in the process of being built. Candles were the only means of illumination as electricity to the camp had not yet been supplied. One soldier wrote home "we have no lights, knives, forks or looking glass."[30] It seems Clipstone Camp added new dimensions to the life of these soldiers.

No cheering crowds greeted the soldiers, only the clang of hammers, and the noise of toiling engines.[31] Mansfield people were denied the opportunity to welcome the troops when the military authorities decided they would alight at Edwinstowe Station not Mansfield. The decision taken was to cause less disruption to the busy market town. Nevertheless it left both the soldiers and the town folk feeling ignored. This, however, was soon forgotten as Mansfield was invaded by thousands of soldiers, and hospitality became of paramount importance. The sight of soldiers soon became a way of life.

**Soldiers walking through the village of Forest Town**

Despite the size of the Clipstone Camp, on occasions there were additional tented camps in the area extending from Mansfield to Clipstone.

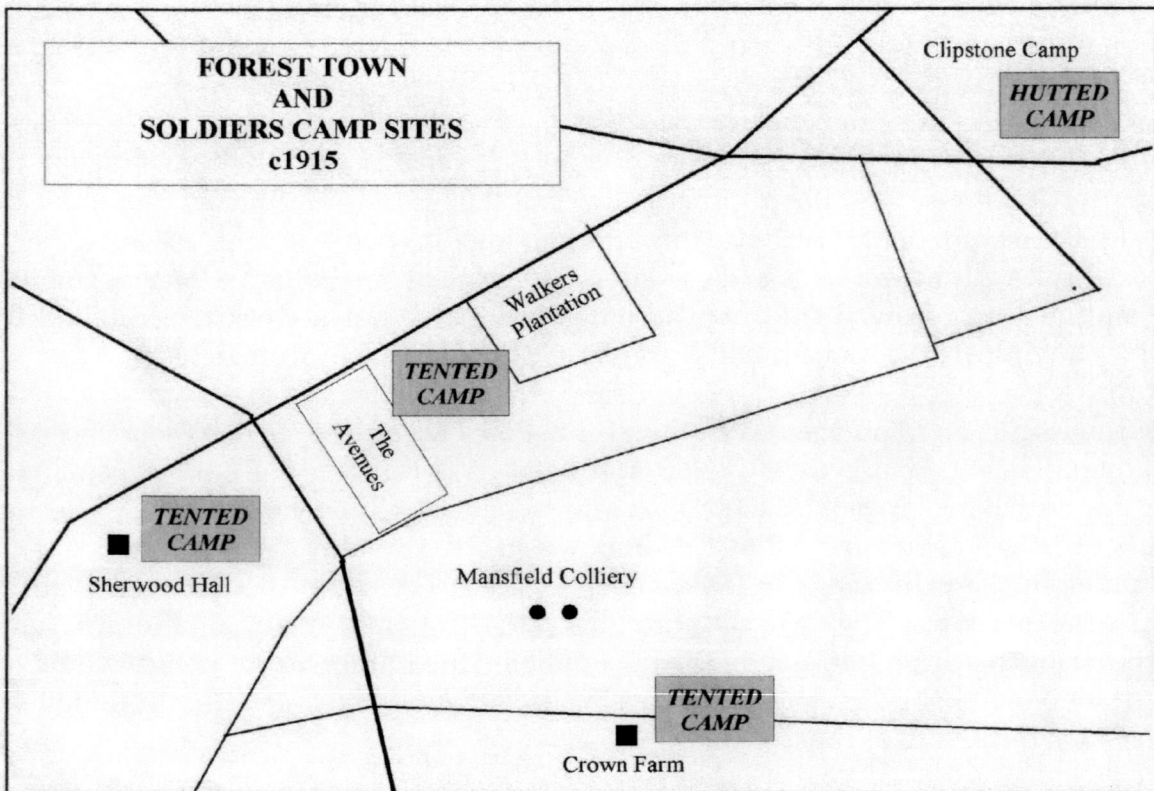

In July 1915 two divisions of the Army Service Corps left Derby on route for Clipstone, these comprised of around 1,000 men, with wagons and horses. The weather was not good and initially the men were quartered in tents, some in the main camp and others in a field adjoining Sherwood Hall, a large country house on the Mansfield side of Forest Town.[32]

The Sherwood Hall Estate in possession of the Bolsover Colliery Company was taken over as the headquarters of the Northern Command. Crown Farm in the tenancy of James Newton also had officers billeted in the house while there were soldiers under canvas in the paddock.[33]

At one time 2,000 men were in tents at Walkers Plantation on the Clipstone Road. The disposal of refuse and inadequate sanitary arrangements from this camp were considered to be a danger to the health of the troops and to the inhabitants of Forest Town which adjoined Walkers Plantation.[34] Unlike the hutted camp at Clipstone the canvas camps were temporary. Nevertheless, they generated both work and expenditure for the local authorities.

Tents in Walkers Plantation with Mansfield (Crown Farm) Colliery in the background.

Tents in Walkers Plantation. Forest Town's 'Avenue' houses can be seen to the right of the picture

The need for vast armies had never been envisaged so it is understandable that the establishing of additional camps created problems. In July 1915 questions were asked in the House of Commons about a rail link to Clipstone Camp. It was revealed that a connection from the newly constructed Mansfield Railway was considered when the Clipstone site was surveyed the previous October. However 'It was decided the cost was too great and the railway would take too long to construct'.[35] Mr Hume-Williams asking the questions of the Under Secretary of War said the railway link would have cost a few hundred pounds and the roads had been damaged to the extent of £6,000. In conclusion he was informed that the camp was now serviced by a railway.[36] The rail connection, however, was for goods only, and it was October 1917 before soldiers benefited from a passenger service to the camp.

It is difficult to assess the number of soldiers in the area at any given time. Initial estimates of the number of men to be stationed at the camp vary between 20,000 and 30,000 though no official statistics are available. Soldiers letters and postcards sometimes revealed numbers. June 1915 - 'there are about 20,000 here at present... there are to be 80,000 soon.'[37] - June 1916 'There is about 60,000 men stationed here.'[38]

Throughout the war, (and even afterwards when the camp was used as a demobilisation centre), there was a vast migration of soldiers in and out of the locality. They came from places near and far, and included the Regiments of the Royal Fusiliers, King's Own Yorkshire Light Infantry, and the Sherwood Foresters. There were men from Bedfordshire, Essex, Middlesex, Scotland and elsewhere. They came to Clipstone before moving to other camps in England and France.[39]

Clipstone Camp transformed the once peaceful countryside: now it vibrated with the sound of men shouting, of marching feet, horses hooves, bugles and gunfire. The noise could be heard for miles around. Consideration was given to the townspeople of Mansfield in as far as the bugles ceased playing when the marching soldiers arrived at Pecks Hill on the outskirts of town.[40]

Photographers with an eye for business enthusiastically recorded many aspects of the camp and the soldiers, making them into post cards for sale. Post cards in the years of World War One, were the easiest means of communication, enabling soldiers to write a short message to their families and friends often with a relevant picture of their regiments, their activities or the huts they lived in.

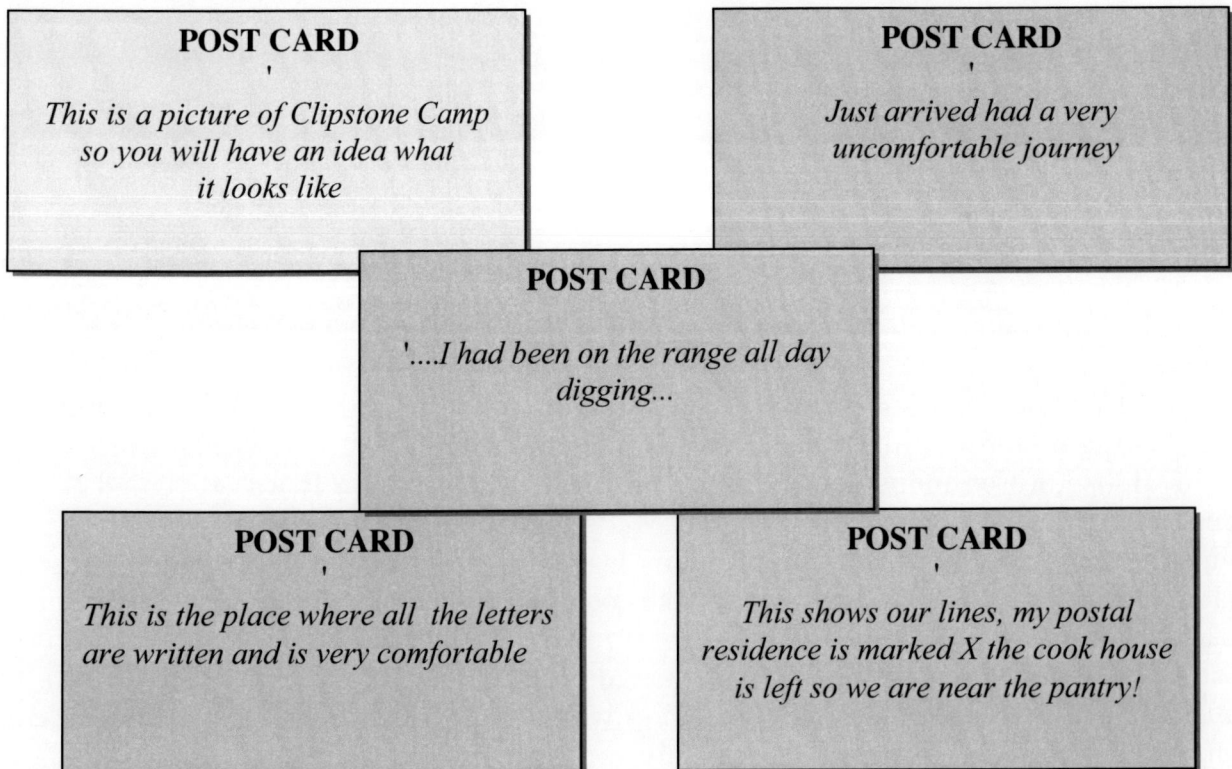

**POST CARD**

*This is a picture of Clipstone Camp so you will have an idea what it looks like*

**POST CARD**

*Just arrived had a very uncomfortable journey*

**POST CARD**

*'....I had been on the range all day digging...*

**POST CARD**

*This is the place where all the letters are written and is very comfortable*

**POST CARD**

*This shows our lines, my postal residence is marked X the cook house is left so we are near the pantry!*

The message on the back of this post card sent from Clipstone Camp 27th July 1915 reads '*I thought you might like to have a photo of the Regt. Of course you cannot see a quarter of us. It was taken as we returned from Church Parade. R.*'

The sight of soldiers marching, just as today, attracted many onlookers and encouraged young lads to try their hand at marching as can be seen in this post card.

Away from the town many of the training activities could be observed, photographers recorded some of them and the local newspapers kept its readers informed of the progress and activities within the camp.

**Soldiers digging trenches or clearing heather.**

In May 1915 when the camp was still being established, the Royal Fusiliers training incorporated improving the camp facilities for the soldiers still to arrive. One improvement that does not appear to fall in the category of military training was gardening. A letter John Chesshire of the 23rd Battalion wrote to his wife on the 21st June 1915 included a drawing of the hut garden they were making. Additionally he has shown bracken and ling [heather] illustrating the terrain the huts were built on.

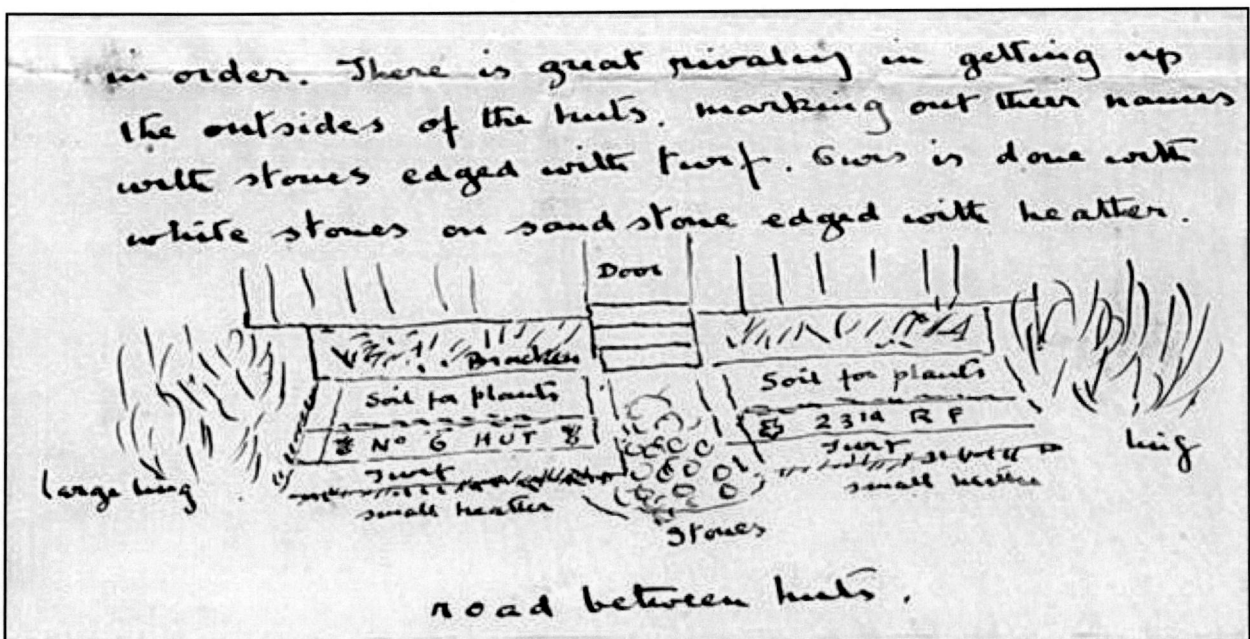

Many of the UPS soldiers had independent incomes and would have been in a position to finance this attempt at 'home improvement'. In contrast, the Mansfield Chronicle informed its readers how squads of men were training by lunging at bags of straw with bayonets, leaping into trenches and crawling along in the undergrowth.[41] The activities of the soldiers altered the surrounding landscape by the digging of trenches. Miniature firing ranges were excavated at Rufford, three miles from the camp.[42] Long marches of up to 25 miles were part of the soldiers itinerary. The country roads and lanes of the area suffered extensive damage from their heavy boots, and the air was choked with dust.

Dust was not the only problem. During the summer months heath fires were a common occurrence near the camp. When this happened alarms were sounded and men armed with rakes and shovels hurried to the burning area. The fires became the focus of humour amongst the soldiers and the subject of a poem printed in 'The Pow Wow' the journal of the UPS Brigade. The last lines read;

'Until we reach the blaze and thither run,
To put it out we eagerly yearn!
But realise it can't be done,
Sit down instead and watch the dam thing burn.'[43]

Life in the camp was enlightened by concert parties provided by the members of various regiments and people from the local towns and villages. Religious services were held, and huts for various denominations were erected in the camp, each at a cost to the particular organisation. The sign of the Red Triangle symbolised the presence of the Young Men's Christian Association (YMCA). Under their emergency war work fund they provided many facilities for the soldiers, including free writing paper and envelopes.[44] Clipstone Camp had three YMCA Huts.

Y.M.C.A. I CLIPSTONE CAMP

The first one opened on 10th July 1915, and by the end of that month, 26,432 letters, plus 4,690 post cards and nearly 100 parcels had been dealt with.[45] For the soldiers letters and postcards were the only means of communication with their friends and families. This subsequently increased the workload of the Mansfield Post Office. As a result extra postal collections were refused to the villages around Mansfield.[46]

The second YMCA Hut was completed in September and the third in November the same year when the Duke of Portland officially opened all three huts.[47] These were strategically placed near the corners of this triangular shaped camp. The three huts were erected by Messrs Bunting and Son of Mansfield, and the cost of the huts excluding furniture was in the region of £2,500. Firms such as Sherwood Colliery (Mansfield) and Player and Sons (Nottingham) contributed to the funding of the huts. At the official opening tribute was paid to the work of the YMCA and all the people, both nationally and locally, that helped.[48]

Throughout the life of the camp many events and expansions took place. Huts from different denominations were added including the Church Army (April 1916), Freemasons (Sept.1916,) Free Church (1917), also for the WAACs (1918).

It has been suggested that prior to a church being erected at the camp St Alban's Church at Forest Town was known as the Garrison Church. However after an appeal by the Bishop of Southwell to churches in the diocese a Garrison Church was built at the camp in 1916. The wooden church built on Gothic lines was opened in April and dedicated to St George the Martyr, the patron saint of soldiers, by the Bishop of Southwell.[49] The church was furnished with several gifts of furniture, the most impressive would have been the carved communion table designed by Mr A S Buxton (headmaster of Mansfield School of Art). It was carved by S E Bevis of G R Cooper Ltd., Mansfield, from oak that was the gift of the Duke of Portland. The involvement of young people was also noted as the service book was presented by the children of Beeston.[50]

**St George's Church in the process of being built**

After the death of Kitchener in June 1916, a memorial service at the camp was attended by 1,200 soldiers.[51] It is not known if this was held in the church or on an open parade ground.

Another permanent addition to the camp in 1916 was the military hospital built by Wm Moss Brothers Ltd of Loughborough.[52] This had had 365 beds, an operating theatre, mortuary, administration block, and staff accommodation.[53] From October 1915 to May 1916 regular adverts appeared in the Derby Daily Telegraph (and possibly other newspapers) for a workforce to build this hospital.

*Derby Daily Telegraph 17th November 1915 Carpenters 10½d per hour, Bricklayers 10½d per hour, Painters 8½d per hour, Navvies, 7d to 8d per hour, Labourers 6½d to 7d per hour. Wanted at the new Military Hospital Clipstone Camp. Apply Moss & Sons office on the Duke of Portland's Private Road.*

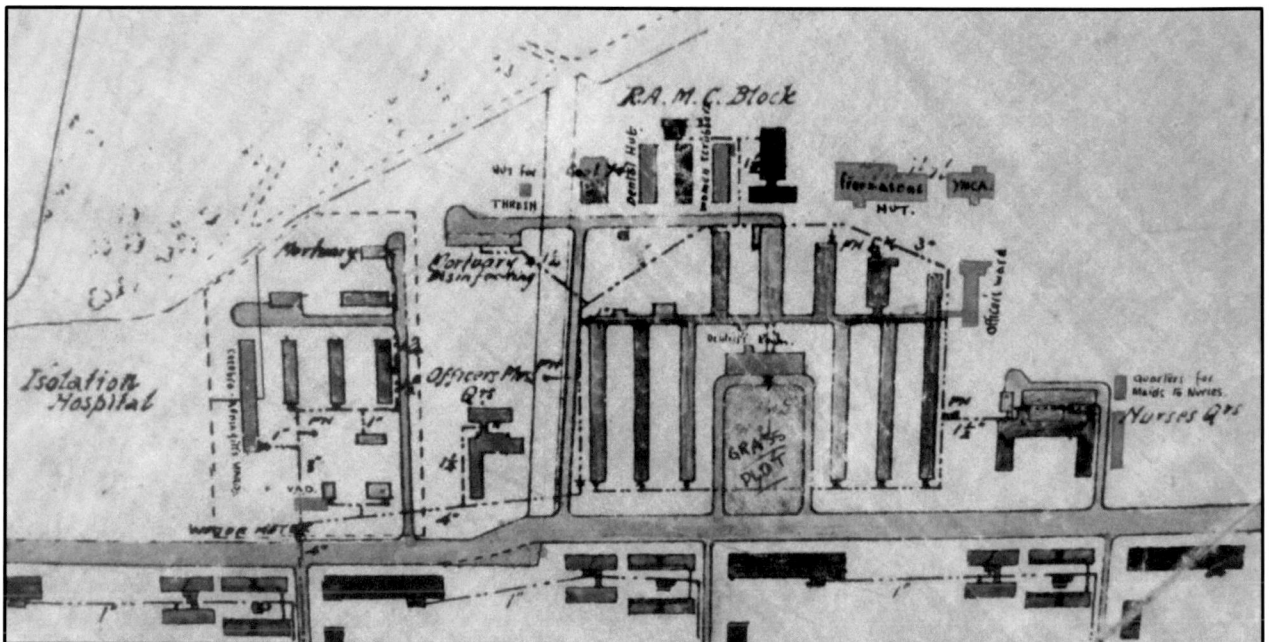

**The Military Hospital Clipstone Camp**

**The plan includes - Isolation Hospital, Cerebro Meningitis Ward, Mortuary, Mortuary Disinfecting area, Dental Hut, Officers Ward, Officers Mess Quarters, Nurses & Nurses Maids Quarters, VAD Hut, Women Scrubbers Hut, RAMC Block, Freemasons Hut and YMCA Hut.**

For patients at the camp hospital, a recreation hut was given by the Masonic Lodges of Nottinghamshire in September 1916. This hut would seat 300 people and was chiefly for the convalescence of wounded soldiers.[54] An extension to this hut was added in June 1918 by the YMCA to provide overnight accommodation for relatives of soldiers in the hospital.[55]

Official documentation has not been found listing facilities available to the soldiers, and these have been discovered through photographs and the camp map. Close scrutiny of the map reveal amenities such as the Post Office (as apposed to YMCA buildings - see photo page 39). Banks including Barclays and London City & Midland also shops both in the camp and on the perimeter. Interestingly the Garrison Theatre is shown outside the main perimeter of the camp

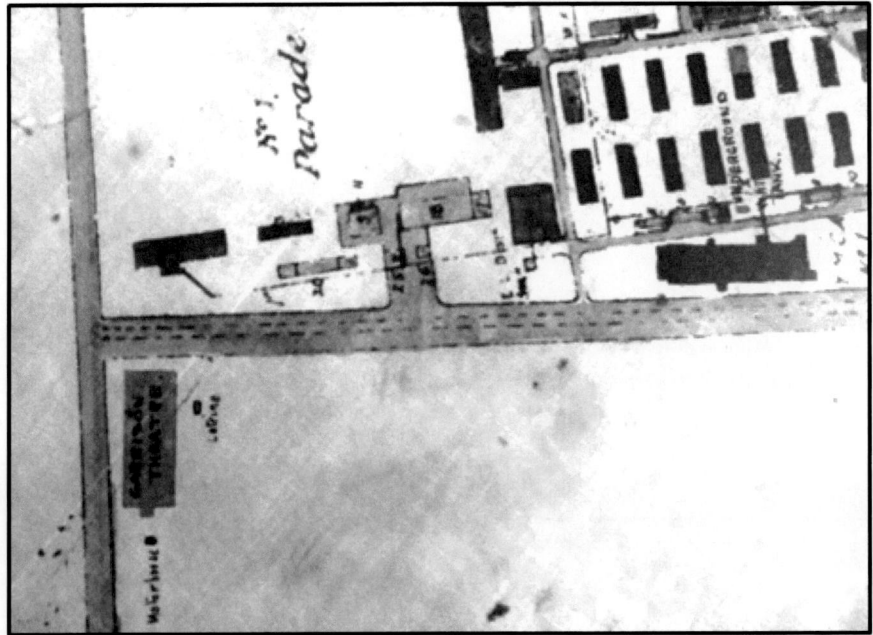

**Garrison
Theatre**

The banks are more conveniently situated nearer to all the soldiers 'Lines' as can be seen on the plan below. Highlighted at the top of this is London & Midland Bank, and at the bottom is Barclays' Bank. This section of the map also shows the Salvation Army Hut, Bread Store, B____ Ovens, Sawdust Yard, Mule Shelter.

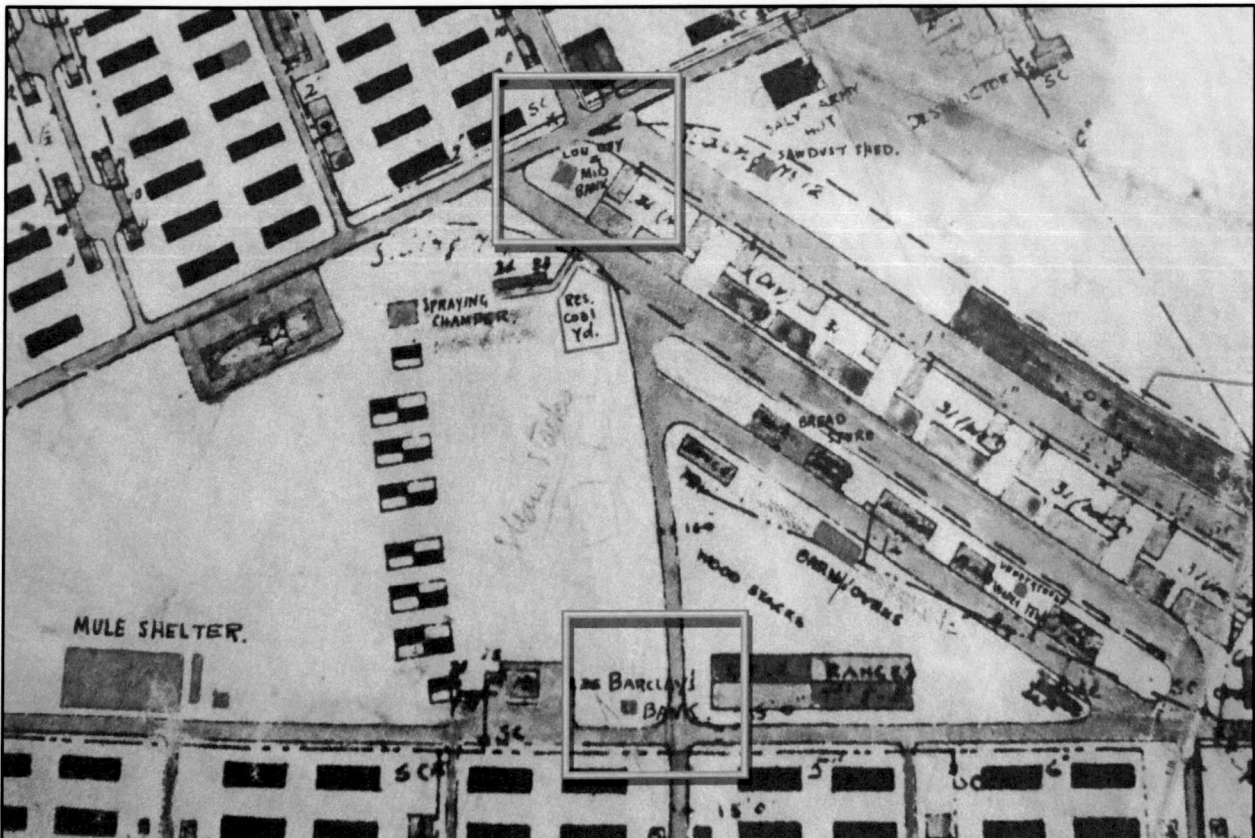

Additional to writing facilities etc to be found in the YMCA huts, items could also be purchased at shops shown in the photographs below. Underneath the words Johnson & Son in the first picture it says 'From Woodcote Park Camp,' that is where the UPS Brigade were before coming to Clipstone. The POW WOW was their newsletter.

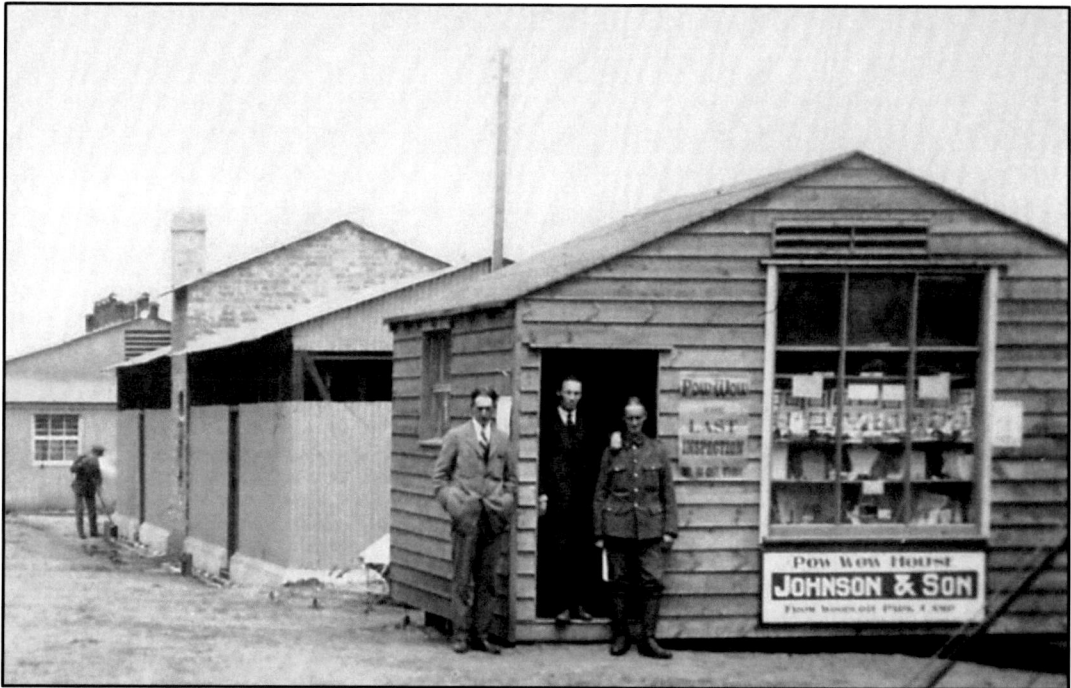

**A Camp shop. 'POW WOW HOUSE'**

**This News Stand/folding shop is from a post card that says 'On the edge of camp.' There is a bicycle on the right of the picture. Newsboys were known to deliver papers to the camp, maybe this is where they sold them.**

The picture of the News Stand also shows the railway line which ran round the camp, referred to as a shunt line.[56] This was connected to the Mansfield railway by a siding branch. In July 1915 it was reported that 'the whole of the material to the camp is now passing over the Mansfield Railway.' [57] Historian J C Fareham notes 'the line provided a regular rail service to Mansfield but could not accommodate major troop movements... a shunt train named Limerick came daily from Tuxford to move heavy loads about the camp.' [58]

Inquests held at the camp illustrate the dangers soldiers faced in training. The accidental death of a soldier shot on the firing range, and one who seized a live grenade in the trenches, both occurred in 1916. A further tragedy took place in September 1917 when a runaway train on the railway resulted in the death of four soldiers from the Royal Scots Fusiliers.[59]

Inevitably with a camp the size of Clipstone and so many soldiers from different backgrounds and skirmishes and tragedies occurring some soldiers would have seen the inside of a guardroom, while others were there on duty.

**Royal Fusiliers outside the Guardroom**

In the last year of the war, a number of Young Soldiers Battalions were stationed at Clipstone Camp,[60] also members of the WAACs. The addition of women in the camp no doubt brought further changes to this hutted encampment, although very little is to be found on this. For them and just people who visited, the size of the camp must have been overwhelming.

People did visit Clipstone Camp from near and far, some were local dignitaries others from soldiers home towns such as the Lord Mayor of Bradford who visited and reviewed the West Yorkshire Regiments stationed there in January 1916,[61] and the

Bishop of Sheffield on the 20th Feb 1916.[62] They would all leave with their own impressions. One visitor from Derbyshire in 1918 wrote 'you can go three miles between the huts, we did not have time, talk about being on Crich Stand [in Derbyshire], it was rough and cold.'[63]

After the war the camp became one of the biggest dispersal centres in the demobilisation organisation.[64] In March 1920 the rear parties of the 16th HLI 53rd Gordons and 15th East Surreys left the camp leaving approximately 100 men of all ranks stationed there.[65] Inevitably the camp closed and the huts were sold to be used as village halls, churches and living accommodation. The area entered a new phase in history as the building of the colliery village recommenced.

**Written on the back of this post card is *F. Behagg at Clipstone Camp, Xmas/15.*
He was a sorting clerk and telegrapher at GPO Clipstone Camp.[66]
This is believed to be the camp post office, and the X under the man in civilian
clothing suggests this is F. Behagg.**

# End Notes

1    The History Of The Royal Fusiliers "UPS" :University And Public Schools Brigade,(1917) Chap. 5
2    Now known as Kings Clipstone.
3    Duke of Portland, *Men, Women and Things,*(1937) pp 228-247
4    Warsop & District Almanac 1915
5    No relevant information has been found in the various Portland Collections or in records of the Bolsover Colliery Company.
6    P Simpkin *Kitchener's Army,*(Manchester 1988).p 237
7    TNA: PRO WO 162/3
8       ibid.
9    Evident in the winter months at Sherwood Pines Forest Park, Clipstone, owned by the Forestry Commission.
10   TNA: PRO WO 162/3
11   NA DC/MW 1/3/4/6        1 Dec. 1914
12      ibid.                1 Dec. 1914
13      ibid.               21 Dec. 1914
14      ibid.                7 Dec. 1914
15   N.A.O. DC/M/1/1/2/4    13 Sep. 1915
16      ibid.               15 Jan. 1915
17   N.A.O. DC/M/1/1/23      9 Apr. 1915
18   Mansfield Museum and Art Gallery, Temporary Exhibition Aug. 1997.
19   N.A.O. DC/M/1/1/24      5 Aug. 1915
20   Mansfield Reporter     12 Mar. 1915  p. 8 col. 5
21   The History Of The Royal Fusiliers "U.P.S." :University And Public Schools Brigade,(1917) Chap. 5
22      ibid.
23    Hansard *HC Deb 14 July 1915 vol 73 cc839-40W* 839W
24   Mansfield Reporter     12 Mar. 1915  p. 8 col. 5.
25   This plan was discovered in private hands in 1999 and has since been deposited in the TNA September 2005.
26   Mansfield Chronicle    26 Aug. 1915  p 1 col.1/2
27   The History Of The Royal Fusiliers "U.P.S." :University And Public Schools Brigade,(1917) p. 82
28      ibid               p. 84
29      ibid.              p. 90
30   Letter from John Chesshire 27 Jun. 1915
31   The History Of The Royal Fusiliers "U.P.S." :University And Public Schools Brigade,(1917) p. 88
32   Derby Daily Telegraph    8 Jul. 1915
33   Oral History, John Newton.
34   N.A.O. DC/MW 1/3/4/6   26 Jul. 1915   & 27 Sep.15
35   Mansfield Chronicle    15 Jul. 1915  p. 1 col. 7
36      ibid.              15 Jul. 1915  p. 1 col. 7
37   Letter from John Chesshire [sic] 27 Jun. 1915
38   Letter from George Henry Waters 1916.
39   James E.A.*British Regiments* 1914-1918,(1978) pp 58-111
40   Oral History, Mrs Brown.
41   Mansfield Chronicle    10 Jun. 1915  p. 1 col. 4
42   The History Of The Royal Fusiliers "U.P.S." :University And Public Schools Brigade,(1917) p. 93
43   MLSL Pow Wow. No 27 11 Jun. 1915   p. 2
44   T Allen 'At The sign of the Red Triangle,' Picture Postcard Monthly, Jul. 1997, pp 10-11
45   Mansfield Chronicle    26 Aug.1915   p.1.col. 1
46   NA DC/MW 1/3/5/4       26 Jul. 1915
47   Mansfield Chronicle    25 Nov. 1915
48      ibid.              25 Nov. 1915  p.7 col. 1-4
49   Linneys Almanac                1917
50   Mansfield Chronicle    27 Apr. 1916
51      ibid.              15 Jun. 1916  p. 2  col. 1
52      ibid.               6 Apr. 1916   see Tribunals.
53   Sale Catalogue 6th September  1921

[54]   Mansfield Chronicle       14 Sep.1917  p. 5 col. 5
[55]   Mansfield Advertiser       7 Jun.1918  p. 2 col. 5
[56]   This can be seen on the camp plan.
[57]   The Railway News       17 Jul.1915
[58]   J C Fareham  *Clipstone Camp.*
[59]   Mansfield Chronicle,       20 Sep.1917  p. 7 col. 2
[60]   M. Marples, Personal research papers.
[61]   Linneys Almanac       1917
[62]     ibid.       1917
[63]   Letter in possession of David Brown written by his mother, to her fiancé Fred.
[64]   Mansfield Reporter     26 Mar. 1920  p. 4 col. 2
[65]     ibid.       26 Mar. 1920  p. 4 col. 2
[66]   Information on James Frederick Behagg can be found in the 1911 Census at March, Cambridgeshire, also on findmypast, Ancestry & CWG web sites.

Filling palliasses with straw -
one aspect of life at Clipstone Camp

# 4 - CAMP LIFE

The vast wooden hutted military training camp of Clipstone Camp which was established near Mansfield in the Nottinghamshire countryside was just one that many soldiers would experience throughout the period of WW1. Initially when the first soldiers arrived in May 1915 the camp was still being set up and facilities were sparse. How this experience can be compared to what the soldiers encountered in the war torn areas of France and elsewhere can only be surmised.

The soldiers that came to Clipstone Camp were from a wide variety of backgrounds and places. The terrain around the camp was very different to the towns and open countryside where many of the soldiers had lived before enlisting. Some had never seen a coal mine and the nearby Mansfield (Crown Farm) Colliery was a popular attraction for some soldiers as the Mansfield Reporter on the 21st May 1915 told its readers:-

> *'The machinery and workings of a coal pit, so close to their new home, naturally became of interest to them. The officials of the pit good naturedly complied with many requests to afford a visit to the underground coal stores of Notts. Officers and men have been caged and dropped into the bowels of the earth by scores, and one day no less than 109 availed themselves of the opportunity. The visitors have been greatly interested and have learnt much, and warmly expressed their appreciation of the trouble taken by hard worked deputies in explaining the details of getting coal from its bed to the surface. Owing to the popularity of 'going down' it has been decided to appropriate Wednesday evening to the 'cheap trip'.*

This took place in the first few days of Clipstone Camp, and the war was still in its infancy. Just how long such trips down Mansfield (Crown Farm) Colliery continued is unknown.

Soldiers soon had a taste of the fresh air around Clipstone when they went on long route marches of up to 25 miles along the country roads, and in the surrounding forests. Dust was always a problem on unmade roads and lanes, more so when the heather had been on fire. On 15th July 1915 the Mansfield Chronicle told its readers :-

> *'After trudging across the Forest following a days work there on Monday, Sportsmen [a unit of the Royal Fusiliers] presented a funny appearance as they marched into camp, for the wind that they had been facing had blown the ashes of the burnt heather and bracken onto their faces, and one would have thought that they had been putting in a day at Crown Farm Colliery, so begrimed were they.'*

At times like this the soldiers would have no doubt welcomed the opportunity of going on 'Bathing Parade'. This was to the Vicar Pond [now known as Vicar Water] about half a mile from the camp. The water in Vicar Pond was deep and two men were always on duty in the event of any mishaps.

Vicar Pond with the Boathouse on the right of the picture in the trees.

Vicar Pond - on the reverse of the post card is hand written.
'Bathing Piquet showing boathouse'.

In the early years of the camp a different kind of pond could be discovered among the huts. Men of the UPS Brigade in an attempt to improve their surroundings had made little gardens in front of their huts, some were enclosed with wooden rails and chains, flowers had also been planted. In one case a small ornamental pond was made, this was enhanced with a tessellated pavement made by chipping pieces from  bricks and cementing them in.[1]

The artistic gardens developed into rivalry between the battalions, with some having preference to creative designs using  pebbles, chipped brick and coal laid on beds of sand. One notable design was outside a hut of the King's Royal Rifles where 'a splendid representation of a black cat with the words 'For Luck' had been formed.'[2]

This was all in stark contrast to the work of the digging of trenches, and charging with bayonets at bags of straw suspended from rails or in trenches full of the imaginary enemy.

> *'Squads of about eight men under the keen and critical eye of an instructor, took turns in stabbing these bags during a quick charge of about 80 to 100 yards, and gruelling work it was under a broiling sun, chasing through the scrub for about a dozen yards, then lunging with a bayonet at a bag suspended from a pole, jumping in a trench, charging another row of bags, then up and at some enemy supposed to be firing from behind a bank of a second trench, over this trench and a short sprint through the heather.'[3]*

The above was recorded on a fine day, however it was also noted that in the early months of the camp torrents of rain resulted in leaking huts making the interiors very uncomfortable. For the Navvies Brigade unfortunate enough to have been under canvas in fields near Forest Town 'the rain and boisterous wind played havoc... practically all of the tents were completely or partially blown over.' While men attempted to re-erect the tents, the officers were taken to the nearby Forest Town Institute for refuge.[4] That was in July 1915 when hutted accommodation on the Clipstone Camp site was still being erected and the need for canvas tents pitched in local fields was still required.

Additional to living quarters, specific huts were provided at the camp by various religious denominations, such as the YMCA, the Church Army, Salvation Army, Wesleyan Methodists, and possibly others. These served a number of purposes, and allowed the soldiers to make contact with people of the same faith. They could communicate and share their fears and inner conflict as the responsibility of defending their country opposed the Christian teaching of 'thou shalt not kill'.[5] Those soldiers who professed to have no faith could find solace and comfort in these huts. For the local volunteers who worked there, it answered a need and gave a distraction from their own personal traumas of the war.

The YMCA huts provided a concert hall, rest rooms, refreshment counters, canteen, games (including billiard tables), reading facilities, also a savings bank and a Post Office.[6] Free writing paper and envelopes were provided by the YMCA, and a wide variety of postcards featuring the camp were also on sale.[7] The photograph below shows the inside of YMCA Hut No 1, with writing paper on the tables. Three wooden post boxes are on a table to the left. The chairs in the front of the picture are possibly facing towards a stage in readiness for a concert or similar.

The YMCA huts were run by volunteers, some would own autograph books, small hard backed books with coloured pages, and they would ask people to sign them.

Signatures, verses and drawings have survived in some autograph books. Many are dated and some like the page illustrated opposite have where they were written 'Clipstone Camp Hut 1 (see top right).

George C Dunstan (bottom signature) was known to be the YMCA Camp Leader, the other two may have been staff in the hut.

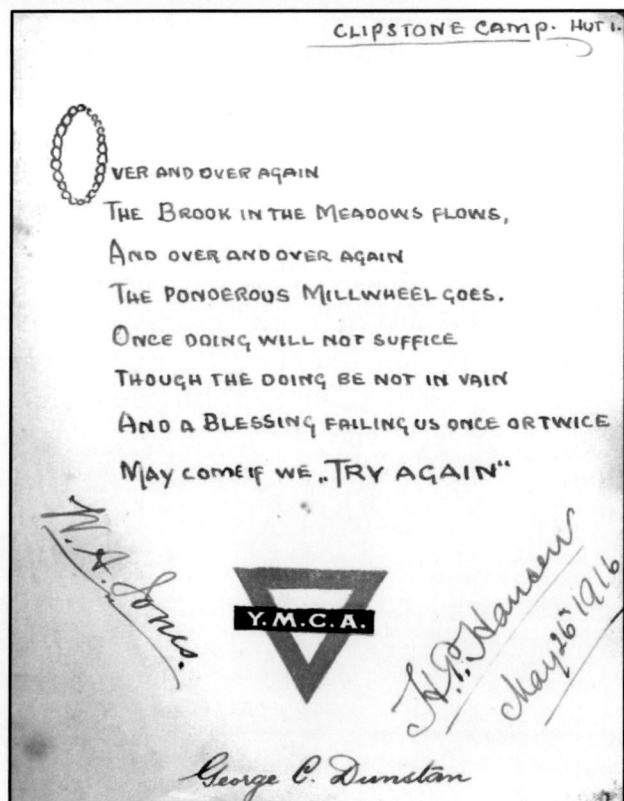

CLIPSTONE CAMP. HUT 1.

Over and over again
The Brook in the Meadows flows,
And over and over again
The Ponderous Millwheel goes.
Once doing will not suffice
Though the doing be not in vain
And a Blessing failing us once or twice
May come if we "Try Again"

Y.M.C.A.

George C. Dunstan

Outside a YMCA hut showing soldiers with their post and also civilian workers - one is just a young lad.

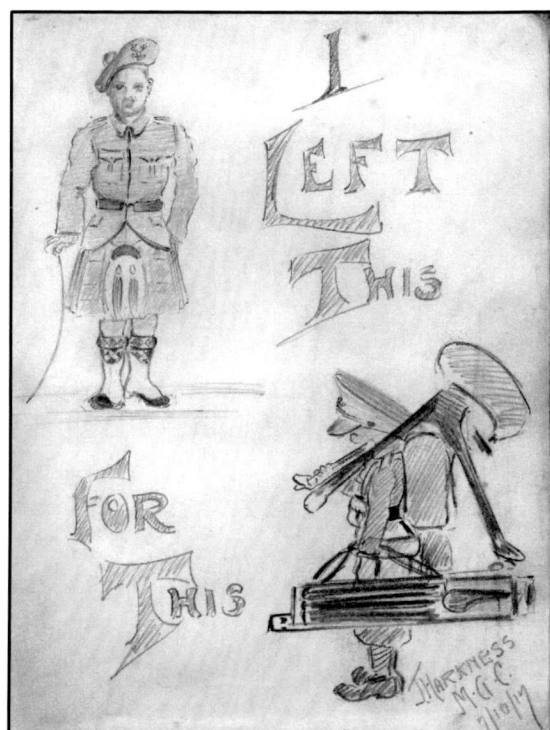

On the above photograph the soldiers have no doubt been encouraged to look cheerful for the camera. However sketches done by some soldiers in autograph books give an insight into their military lives, and thoughts.

This informative sketch drawn by Pte J S Willock Royal Fusiliers
dated July 1915, is on a page in Lily Chadwick's autograph book.
Poignantly he adds 'Writing Home.'

Soldiers when writing home often referred to the events on the camp such as parades or inspections. The picture below shows masses of soldiers from left to right facing the lone figure stood at a higher level. Handwritten on the back of the photograph are the words 'Brigade inspection by Sir Bruce Hamilton at Clipstone Camp. Sir Bruce Hamilton then in command of troops under the Northern Command'.

A soldier sending this post card to an address in Glasgow (June 1916) wrote on the back "This is a photo of a 'drum head' service. You can see of course that it is not a Protestant or rather not a Presbyterian church parade, you can see the parson in the centre, clothed in 'white samite - mystic wonderful.' He is Church of England. With the exception of the Aberdeen Minister in Chatham I have never come across in the army a Presbyterian parson."

His message indicates how some soldiers would welcome a connection to their own faith wherever they were situated. Some when possible would specifically attend services at various churches and chapels in and around Mansfield.

Christmas was a time when the soldiers welfare received extra special consideration, not only in the local churches and at the Mansfield YMCA but on the camp site itself. The local newspapers such as the Mansfield Chronicle were keen to report these events. In December 1916 a large 'family' type party was held for the staff and soldiers who frequented the Church Army Hut. The Duke of Portland and local tradesmen had provided refreshments, smokes and fruit. Possibly the largest festivities were held on Boxing Day (1916) in YMCA Hut No 1 when a 1,000 soldiers were catered for in two sittings beginning at 5pm. Preparations had started in the morning when lady helpers from Mansfield had begun the great task of making sandwiches and packing the food into bags for the 1000 soldiers. The hut was colourful with decorations and a centre piece was of flags of the allied nations. Long lines of white covered tables, had centre decorations of sprigs of evergreens. A bag of food was set at each place and cigarettes and fruit were also given to each soldier. Special Christmas greetings plus donations for the event, had been received from the Lord Mayor of Bradford, the Mayor of Halifax and the Chairman of Elland District Council. These were read out to the men, many of them were from the Yorkshire battalions stationed at the camp at that time, they responded with great cheers pleased to know they had not been forgotten by people back home.

Additionally the soldiers did not forget the folks back home as the five words hand written on the back of the Christmas at Clipstone 1917 photograph reveal - 'For Dear Old Mum, Hal.'

Christmas at Clipstone 1917

Christmas at Clipston 1914

The inscription on the back of this picture, says 'This is a photo of our cake and the cooks who made it - made in the shape of a house.' It could be suggested there is more to this than just the baking of the cake as it warranted being displayed in front of the Union Flags and draped with garlands.

An unknown event suggesting entertainment and fun.

Away from the rigours of training and the unknown horrors of war many of them would eventually endure, the morale of the soldiers was kept up with entertainment such as concerts from a wide variety of artists who visited the camp or were stationed there. In September 1915 it was reported that in YMCA Hut No 1 several 'singsongs' had been arranged by the soldiers to while away the evenings. Concert parties from Mansfield, Newark and Huthwaite also planned visits over the next few weeks.[8] They entertained the soldiers by singing musical solos and duets, such as 'Somewhere a Voice is Calling' and 'The Hills of Home'. Piano, trumpet and cornet recitals were also part of the concert parties programmes.

In contrast the entertainment provided in the Church Army Hut in April 1916 was noted as being of songs, recitations, ventriloquisms, impersonations, club swings etc., These were performed by Lieut. S G Saville, Lieut. E W Pearson, Lieut. G C Henrick, Sergt. Coxhead (club swinging), Pte. Jones (ventriloquist), Lance-corpl. Robinson (comic), Pte. Thorpe (impersonation), Bandsman Knighton, Pte. Thorpe, Pte. Harris, Pte. Acton, Pte. Ball, Pte. Rhodes, Pte. Coates, Pte. Croucher, Nurse Footit, Nurse Plant and Sergeant Fairweather who had arranged the concert.[9] It is interesting to learn the names of two nurses who were possibly stationed at the camp hospital.

Soldiers participating in concerts and sporting events away from the camp are well documented, however the only reference to sporting activities/exercises taking place on the camp itself are in photographs, seen in the examples below.

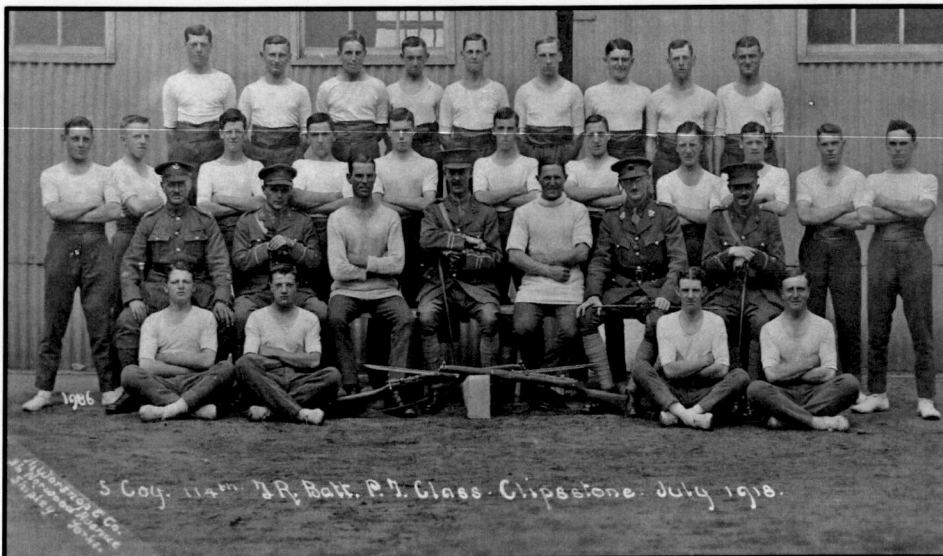

5 Coy.
114th TR Batt.
PT Class
Clipstone
July 1918

Reg$^t$. Football Team
52nd Notts. & Derbys.
Clipstone
Nov. 1918

Heavy Weight Team. 5th Batt. Royal Fusiliers Clipstone May 1919

Camp life also had its darker side, for it was not just the knowledge that once soldiers were sent off to fight in the war that they would lose friends and colleagues, for some it happened during their time at Clipstone. One of the first known deaths occurred in June 1915 when 25 year old Private Robert Louis Garside of the 21st Royal Fusiliers was taken seriously ill at the camp. He had to be moved to Bagthorpe Isolation Hospital, Nottingham where he died of meningitis on the 29th June. He was buried with full military honours at Nottingham Church Cemetery, and the funeral procession included 180 officers and men of the Royal Fusiliers.[10]

On the 2nd July 1915 Cpl. John Henry Richardson of the 22nd Royal Fusiliers was knocked down and fatally injured by a motor car on Clipstone Road as he was walking back to the camp from Mansfield late at night. He left a widow and young child, in those early days of the war she would never have expected to lose her husband in this way.[11]

Over the next few years, there were other tragedies that involved soldiers and motor vehicles. There were suicides, and cases of drowning, Sapper William Davis aged 25, No 2 Tunnelling Depot, Royal Engineers had only been at the camp one day when he was found drowned in the River Maun in May 1916.[12]

Additionally there were deaths as a result of training and one such tragedy was on the 11th April 1916 when William Henry Gillott, a private in the 1/4 York & Lancaster Regiment and other soldiers were in a hut on the rifle range at Clipstone Camp. Rifle practise was proceeding at the time and a bullet came through the door of the hut, and struck Pte. Gillott. He was taken to the military hospital where he died a few hours later from shock and haemorrhage.[13]

In September 1917 four soldiers of the Royal Scots Fusiliers died as a result of a train accident at the camp. All were laid to rest in their native hometowns in Scotland.

Deaths such as those above and many others at the camp resulted in inquiries and investigations of the cause with these being reported in local newspapers.

While the total number of soldiers who passed through Clipstone Camp is unknown, estimates have been given of upwards of 20,000 to 30,000 at any one time, and with a constant changeover of regiments this equates to a staggering number which is difficult to calculate with any accuracy.

In the early months of the war many of those arriving there would have been fresh faced young soldiers who were eager to fight for King and Country and the camp and its surroundings would have been an accepted place on their journey. In the latter years after the end of the war when the camp became a dispersal centre, the battle weary men arriving there would have had very little interest in their surroundings, they just wanted to return to civilization. For them Clipstone Camp was just the name of the place stamped on their demobilisation papers.

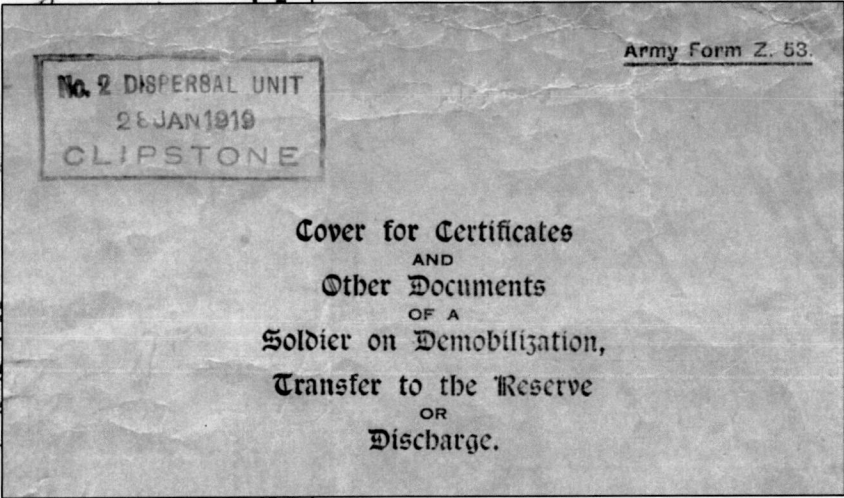

Sample of Discharge Paper and Document Envelope both showing Clipstone

# END NOTES

| | | | |
|---|---|---|---|
| 1 | Mansfield Chronicle | 10 Jun. 1915 | |
| 2 | ibid. | 15 Jul. 1915 | |
| 3 | ibid. | 10 Jun. 1915 | |
| 4 | ibid. | 22 Jul. 1915 | |
| 5 | *Exodus*, Ch.20 v.13.Holy Bible King James version. | | |
| 6 | Mansfield Chronicle | 25 Nov.1915 p. col. 1-4 | |
| 7 | Postcards of Clipstone Camp are now collectors' items. | | |
| 8 | Mansfield Chronicle | 9 Sep. 1915 & 21 October 1915 | |
| 9 | ibid. | 13 Apr. 1916 | |
| 10 | ibid. | 8 Jul. 1915 War Graves of the British Empire Nottinghamshire p. 35 | |
| 11 | ibid. | 8 Jul. 1915 & Commonwealth War Graves Commission. | |
| 12 | ibid. | 5 May. 1916 | |
| 13 | ibid. | 13 Apr. 1916 | |

- 56 -

Happy soldiers

# 5 - THE SOCIAL IMPACT OF CLIPSTONE CAMP

In the late autumn of 1914, the community of Mansfield and area, heard that a large military camp was to be built near their town. They could not, however, have envisaged how much it would infiltrate into their lives and even if they had there was not the time nor opportunity for consultation and protests as happens today when large housing schemes or industrial estates are built.

People in December 1914 were only just adapting to the departure of men from their homes, and their locality, going off to fight in a war in distant lands. The war was four months old and realisation was beginning to dawn that it would not be over by Christmas as was first anticipated. The pressure on young men to enlist and move away was increasing day by day. Employers, church organisations and each local community watched as the war took their male populations away.

Within a short time of local men enlisting news came of men who had been injured. Among them were: Private H Havenhand 2nd Batt Kings Royal Rifles (Big Barn Lane, Mansfield), Private E Savidge RAVC (Clipstone).[1] Private Gladstone Short (Mansfield).[2] J P Houfton in a recruiting speech at the end of November 1914 in Forest Town encouragingly said 356 employees of the colliery [Mansfield] had gone, however he also revealed some had been wounded, two were taken prisoner. He also told of the death of Pte W Cutts (single), and Pte J E Smitheringale and Corporal F J Munnings both married with children.[3]

Families were left behind to cope and adjust. For the people of Mansfield and area this adjustment took on a new emphasis as the building of the Clipstone Camp progressed. The exceptional traffic on the roads, the additional noise and rumours of thousands of soldiers to be stationed at the camp gave a new awareness of the war. The war was not just in a distant land it had come to Mansfield!

Over the next few years communities all over Britain shared in the many aspects of war. Their dead were remembered in homes, the workplace, on memorials in the church, or churchyard. St Alban's Churchyard, Forest Town was the nearest burial place to Clipstone Camp and one nurse and 27 soldiers were laid to rest there.[4] Their deaths occurred from accidents, influenza, bronchitis and pneumonia.[5] Occasionally a soldier was found dead in the flood dykes or river near Clipstone, the implication of accident or suicide being decided at the inquest.

Children were not immune to the horror of war, and the patriotism of military funerals was instilled into the children of the Forest Town School, adjacent to the churchyard. The children and their teachers remained silent as they heard the gun carriage go past, the bugle playing the last post and the graveside gun salute.[6] Local people would join soldiers in the churchyard as they buried their comrades from the camp. For some their grief would also be for their own soldier husband, son, brother who were buried in a distant land.

The importance of marking the soldiers final resting place with lasting memorials encouraged the local mining community to subscribe to a fund for memorial crosses.

These were dedicated in July 1917 in a special service attended by soldiers from the camp, representatives from Mansfield Colliery and a large congregation. There were nine soldiers buried in the churchyard at that time.

Sergt. John Linton (45) Royal Garrrison Artillery.
Rifleman John Simpson (38) 7th Res. West Yorkshire Regiment.
Pte. George Edward Brew (36) 2nd Battallion MGC
Pte. Henry Rosewell (45) RAMS.
Pte. Percy Hudson (33) 6th Reserve Duke of Wellingtons.
Corpl. Arthur [Alfred] Ernest (48) 6th Reserve Duke of Wellingtons.
Pte. William Blakey (28) 7th Reserve Duke of Wellingtons
Pte. Frank Percy Louis Clarke (26) ASC.
Pte. John Symonds (26) 3/5th West Yorks.[7]

Within a few weeks the camp and community were once again united for the burial of a soldier from the camp, that of Sergt. Francis Arthur Orridge. (47) Royal Engineers.

**This postcard has the name of Sergt. Orridge written on the back.
He was buried on the 30th August 1917**

More soldiers burials followed until August 1919. In May 1921 an agreement was made with the then Imperial War Graves Commission and the Churchyard Committee for the maintenance of the war graves, there were now 29. At a date unknown the crosses were replaced by the standard war grave memorials.

The war years were not all sorrow and from the onset of Clipstone Camp in May 1915 the sharing of formal and informal events became a way of life for both the military troops and the local community. The first notable occasion to occur in this way, was the camp open day on the 13th June 1915. Newspaper headlines in the Mansfield Chronicle read:

## The Clipstone Camp
## Royal Fusiliers 'At Home'.
## The Public have a Sunday Afternoon Out.

Curiosity, not respect was the prime factor for most of the civilian population. They turned out in their thousands on a hot Sunday afternoon. It was not just the community around Mansfield who were curious, people travelled from distant places such as Alfreton, Bolsover, Blackwell and Sutton, distances of up to sixteen miles. The road between Mansfield and the camp was congested with people on foot, in pony and traps, wagons and motorcars. The air was thick with the sandy dust from the road surface, it was said to be inches thick in places, but it did not deter the people who were determined to see the camp.

Other military camps such as Ripon, were known to invite the public into the camp for special occasions,[8] however no evidence has been found of other camps hosting an open day similar to the one at Clipstone. G S Flemming, a Salisbury historian suggests the new camps built around Salisbury Plain would not have warranted an introduction to the community as a military presence was in existence long before 1914. Additionally his philosophy that the expansion camps with huge squalid tents would not warrant displaying to the public is logical.[9]

Clipstone Camp was not an expansion camp, it did not consist of huge tents, there were rows and rows of large huts and the people who visited the camp discovered it was on a much larger scale than they had imagined. It covered an expanse wider than the eye could see, and they were of the opinion the camp was not just a temporary arrangement as some had imagined.[10]

The main reason for throwing open the camp was due to a visit of the band of the 1st and 2nd Battalions of the Sherwood Foresters, who had been recruiting in Mansfield and the vicinity in the previous week. Permission to open the camp was given by Brigadier General Gordon Gilmour CVO., CB., DSO., and other officers of the UPS Brigade. While the general public took the opportunity to inspect the camp, the band occupied the parade ground of the 19th Battalion of the Fusiliers and played to entertain the crowds.

While some gathered to listen to the music, many others took the opportunity to investigate the soldiers accommodation and ask questions of the Fusiliers who acted as guides.

Huts as far as the eye can see

The addition of the gardens in front of some huts gave an air of permanent occupation to the visitors. For the soldiers it provided a boost to their morale. Showing the public round the camp offered light relief to the soldiers and their additional humour of 'C View. Apartments', 'To Let' or 'Fortunes Told Here'[11] on various huts, added to the enjoyment of the visitors. For the people of Mansfield and the district around it, the open day at Clipstone Camp gave a different perspective of the war. Temporarily the fighting and the deaths were forgotten. The people saw a place where soldiers could live, train, and have fun. The soldiers were like their

Huts with gardens

own husbands, sons and employees who had recruited for the army, and they could warm to them. The open day was a significant step towards securing good public relations between the camp and the local communities.

The soldiers were quick to visit establishments in Mansfield such as the Grand Theatre, The Palace, (both on Leeming Street) and The Empire (Stockwell Gate). that provided entertainment. They frequented places that offered refreshment, and an extension to the Oriental Cafe on West Gate, provided extra seating accommodation for customers, plus a room with smoking and billiard facilities.

# The Oriental Cafe,

## WEST GATE,

### MANSFIELD.

Such was the impact of soldiers from the camp visiting the YMCA hall in Mansfield it had to extend and use all its available space instead of using just half of it. The upstairs hall offered the opportunity for reading, recreation and music, while the whole of the lower hall was devoted entirely to serving refreshments. With the whole of the building in use they could accommodate 1,500 men. In 1916 alone the YMCA hall served 78,000 meals.[12]

YMCA Hall Church Lane, Mansfield

Financial contributions for the YMCAs work both in Mansfield and at Clipstone Camp was donated from local schools such as Brunts and the Girls' Grammar School. Money also came from individual people including soldiers. One lady sent £15 towards the purchase of a piano for use in the YMCA huts at the camp.[13]

Religious establishments in and around the town were quick to welcome soldiers to worship with them. Soldiers of a strong faith would reciprocate by preaching or playing the organ at an appropriate service. It was said that 'Khaki in the pulpit had become a familiar sight in several of the places of worship, and the announcement that the pulpit was to be occupied by a soldier was sufficient to ensure a large congregation.'[14]

Only occasional reports of soldiers frequenting the public houses are mentioned, however they too would have been well patronised by the men from the camp.[15] They were also visited by soldiers who were patients in the Mansfield Hospital which could cause a problem for the landlords if they disguised their identity. While wounded soldiers had a blue uniform and often a red tie they retained their khaki great coat and cap. It was not unknown for them to borrow a pair of puttees and wrap them over their trousers, button up their great coat and go into a public house requesting a drink. A regulation under the Defence of the Realm Act said:

> No sale of intoxicating liquor should be made at any time to any member of His Majesty's forces who is a patient at a military or voluntary aid hospital.

In June 1916 John Baggaley landlord of The Eagle Tavern, Mansfield was fined heavily when four soldiers from the hospital were discovered drinking on his premises. It was the only charge made against him in the 13 years he had been tenant of the house. On denying knowledge of them being patients it was said that it was a hot day and these men who had their great coats buttoned up to their necks ought to have been given more scrutiny![16]

The presence of soldiers was everywhere, and the hospitality to them was extended into the homes of the people. Appropriately, the male population issued the invitations and the ladies of the house were left to produce the tea.[17] Hospitality was extended to soldiers' families enabling them to be united for short visits.[18] For many people house space was already short but the prospect of a little added income was always welcome.

Even the more fortunate people in the neighbourhood would let their home. People like Mrs Gorton of Walesby Vicarage, who, in September 1915 contacted the agent of the Thoresby Estate, H W Argles, and offered her home for rent while she was in London. Mr Argles was liaison officer in the letting of local accommodation. He replied stating that as 'Clipstone Camp would be filling up, several officers will want nice houses.'[19] Some officers advertised in local newspapers for accommodation for their families:-

---

*Mansfield Chronicle 6th April 1916*

**WANTED**
*Wanted June & July furnished house or rooms for Officer's wife,
and two children, near Clipstone Camp must be country.
Apply Major Murray 3/3 WRF Ambulance, Clipstone*

---

Renting private accommodation in this way not only allowed officers families to live with them. they sometimes had the added advantage of rowing and fishing in private lakes.[20] Such a freedom was denied the ordinary soldiers. Nevertheless, soldiers were given the opportunity of bathing, swimming or rowing at ponds within the vicinity of the camp.

Regular bathing parades were part of the daily routine to Vicar Pond[21] half a mile from Clipstone Camp where soldiers in a boat were ready to rescue any casualties in the deep water.[22] It is doubtful that this was as idyllic as the sketch in the Royal Fusiliers magazine the 'POW WOW' of July 1915 suggests.

**"VICAR'S WATER."**

Various sporting facilities were made available to the soldiers and this gave them the opportunity to integrate with local communities. They could use the Mansfield Baths at times specified for them, and additional use was authorised by the Baths Committee for team races and water polo matches between the different battalions from the camp.[23]

While a planned new sports ground in Mansfield had not been completed, the Forest Town Institute in close proximity to Clipstone Camp quickly offered its first class sports ground, and the privileges of the Institute to the soldiers. The sportsmen amongst the soldiers never dreamt they would have the use of such a sports ground with its first class cricket pitch. This was surrounded by an asphalt sports track, and there was also a bowling green and tennis courts.

On the first Saturday in June 1915 over 300 members of the UPS Brigade were in the grounds watching  cricket played between officers and NCOs and men of the brigade. It was noted that it was the first time 'Varsity Cricket' had been played at Forest Town, [not surprising in a small mining village]. There would be even more opportunities to watch cricketers who had made their name at Cambridge, Oxford, Middlesex, Sussex, Hants, Surrey and other counties. Cricketers who now found themselves in the role of soldiers. Gate money on the day raised £5 for the Red Cross.[24]

The.Institute and Grounds, Forest Town, (J. S. & S. Copyright). 1661.

The arrival of the Sportsmen's Battalions at the camp brought notable football players from places such as Millwall and West Ham, they participated in events played on the Mansfield Football Ground.[25] In peace time football matches were not normally associated with Bank Holiday Monday, however in August 1915 Mansfield people braved the elements to watch a game played between the 'A' and 'B' Companies of the Footballers Battalion.

**A Company**;- Hugall (Clapton Orient) goal; Spencer (Brighton) and Stewart (Watford) backs; Tull (Northampton), Woodhouse (Brighton), and Borthwick (Millwall), half -backs; Roberts (Luton), Williams (Millwall), Jones (Clapton Orient), Gregory (Queens Park). and Barnfather (Croydon Common) forwards.

**B Company**:- Webster (West Ham), goal; Gibson (Notts Forest) and Bullock (Huddersfield), backs; Baker (Plymouth), Scott (Clapton Orient), and Barber (Aston Villa) halfbacks; Sheldon (Liverpool), Coleman (Notts Forest), Foster (Reading), Bailey (Reading), and Goodwin (Exeter City), forwards.

The game proceeded well until rain stopped play just after half time.[26]

Sherwood Golf Course was in close proximity to Clipstone Camp and while much of the area surrounding the greens became a training ground for soldiers, the officers were more fortunate and were given the privilege to use the course itself and play golf. They are reputed to have walked from their quarters and commenced their game at the twelfth hole. In repayment of hospitality, officers at the Camp gave two trophies to the club.[27] A cup was inscribed:

CLIPSTONE CAMP CUP,
PRESENTED TO
THE SHERWOOD FOREST GOLF CLUB,
BY THE GOLFERS AMONGST
THE OFFICERS OF CLIPSTONE CAMP
IN RETURN FOR KINDNESS AND
HOSPITALITY
SHOWN THEM JUNE 1917

And a trophy depicting a kilted Scots soldier has the words:

THE SCOTTISH TROPHY
PRESENTED TO
THE SHERWOOD FOREST GOLF CLUB,
BY THE OFFICERS
OF THE HIGHLAND DIVISION
CLIPSTONE CAMP 1919

**Sherwood Forest Golf Club House**

Despite the constant turnover of troops at the camp, the relationship and sporting activities between the camp and civilians continued throughout the war. Hockey and cricket matches were played between pupils of the Brunts Grammar School in Mansfield and soldiers from the camp.[28] Military personnel assisted in forming a Cadet Corps at the school during the last year of the war.[29]

Forest Town Sports Ground continued to be a popular venue for events. Its close proximity to the camp and the standard of the ground were a decisive factor. When the Institute and Sports Ground were opened in 1908 it was never envisaged that it would be over-run with soldiers, and that Military Sports such as the one that took place in June 1916 would be the cause of great attraction.

## Military Sports
## Highly Successful Meeting at Forest Town

'An interesting afternoon's sport was witnessed in the colliery institute grounds at Forest Town, Mansfield, on Saturday afternoon by a large attendance, the fixture being arranged by the Northern Command Cross Country and Physical Fitness Association.'

The 22 events included several novelties, including

## Sandbag Filling,
## Grenade Throwing,
## Bayonet Disc Carrying,
## Pick-a-Back Wrestling

The flat events were keenly contested, and Pte. Simpson (Duke of Wellington's), and Pte. Kirton (West Yorks) the former in the half-mile and the latter in the 100 and 220 yards, were popular winners.

There was a cross country run of about 5 miles, a one mile cycle race, a sack race, obstacle race and high jump

Music was supplied by the regimental bands.
The Hon. Secretary of the sports was Lieut. E. W. Harris.
Men from the: Duke of Wellington's, York & Lancs., West Yorks., Cyclists, Royal Engineers, KOYLI took part. [30]

Once again the roads around the whole area would have been thronged with people, the majority on foot. It was a social event that could not have been considered at the start of the war.

One recorded sports event took place at the camp itself in July 1918 in connection with the 3rd (Reserve) Battalion of the Machine Gun Corps. A large number of guests and civilians watched both the sports and additional fun events. The music of both the band of the 87th TRBs and the orchestra of the Machine Gun Corps enhanced the day.[31]

Another event known to attract large crowds took place over three days at the beginning of August 1918 as the mood of the country was becoming more relaxed. The venue was grounds on Chesterfield Road in Mansfield This was a Military Gymkhana and Fete and it was in aid of the Machine Gun Corps Prisoner of War Fund.

The Mansfield Chronicle carried a list of people who had subscribed to the expense of this event. Mansfield and District Chamber of Commerce collected the donations which ranged from £25 to 10/- and were given by The Duke of Portland, local businesses and individual people and were in excess of £249. With money raised at the three day event this totalled over £2,000.

DON'T MISS seeing the TRENCH, and DAYLIGHT TRENCH RAID A Wonderful Representation of Modern Warfare.

At the Boxing Marquee Staff-Serg' PAT. O'KE. E, Middle We.. st Champion, will appear daily.

Have Your PHOTO TAKEN on the 25in. Shell.

Many Other Novelties.

At the MILITARY GYMKHANA & FETE
IN AID OF
Machine Gun Corps Prisoners of War Fund.
AUGUST 5th, 6th and 7th, 2.30 p.m. each day.
DON'T FORGET THE AUCTION OF FARM AND DAIRY PRODUCE in the Pig Market, Westgate, Mansfield, at 2.30 p.m., SATURDAY, AUGUST 3rd.

The event named 'Plug Street' had military tournaments, side shows, horsemanship, bayonet fighting, gymnastic display etc. Over the three days thousands of people had the chance of visiting trenches 'specially constructed at much expense and labour in order that Mansfield people might get a glimpse of the life the boys are living out there.' A tour of the trenches on 'Plug Street' took people through and past sleeping bunks, sentries, dug outs, gun emplacements and more.[32] Prior to a very realistic mock raid in which 80 men took part, people were warned there was 'Absolutely no danger, you get the effects without the usual consequences.' While it must have been a thrilling experience for some people, it could have been a disquieting one for those who had family fighting overseas. A souvenir post card of this raid was on sale and it was hoped it would be a memento in years to come - [one has yet to be discovered].

A special highlight that took place one afternoon on the tournament ground was the presentation of the Canadian Ensign to one of the Canadian Forestry Companies that were stationed in the area [just where is unknown]. 'The flag which was the gift of Training Group 'C' of the Machine Gunners was 'broken' at the masthead by Miss Avice Pearson daughter of Col. E F Pearson commanding the MGC, in the presence of a large company which included General _. J Maxwell, Brigadier General Griffiths and the Mayor and Mayoress of Mansfield Mr and Mrs W F Wharmby... Col. Pearson said the MGC felt honoured to have a unit of the splendid Canadian Army serving so closely to them.'[33]

While the Canadians were known to take part in sporting events in both Mansfield and Forest Town it is unknown if they participated in anything at Clipstone Camp itself.

While sporting events were restricted to places with the appropriate facilities, musical and theatrical entertainment took place in a wider area. Anywhere with a large hall could be utilised for performances. Entertainment was provided for the soldiers, and by the soldiers. While some battalions contained professional sportsmen, others had those with musical and acting ability. They participated in many local fund-raising concerts adding to the enjoyment of the public. Similarly, members of the civilian community who were musically talented performed both in the town, and at the camp for the benefit of the soldiers.

One memorable event took place on a Saturday afternoon in March 1917 at the Grand Theatre in Mansfield. This was a concert and sketch put on by the 6th Machine Gun Corps who were stationed at Clipstone Camp. Amongst those present were the Duchess of Portland, the Mayor and Mayoress and Lt. Col. Pearson. The sketch gave an insight into the realities of war depicting, 'just the kind of things that happen in France when a gas attack by the Germans is made.' The sketch was said to be unique in as much it was the first time one like it had been seen on stage. It was written out of experience by Major Houston who had served in France. Pte. Hill, Pte. Collins, Lieut. Alan Frost, Lieut. Castle, RMQS Owen and Lieut. Cregan were members of the cast. A lighter side of the concert consisted of various musical items and a physical training demonstration by NCOs and men of the 4th Battalion. The concert raised £55 for Machine Gunners serving at the Front.[34]

While the camp with its thousands of soldiers had many advantages for the community, and gave rise to plenty of opportunity for socialising, there was also a concern over moral welfare. In December 1914, the Bishop of Birmingham speaking at a recruitment rally in Mansfield warned of the danger of placing temptation in the way of men'.[35]

He was referring to the proposed camp and the massive influx of soldiers about to descend on Mansfield. To the assembled people, he recommended that intoxicating drink should not be given to the soldiers.

> **BISHOP OF SOUTHWELL**
>
> **AND THE**
>
> **NEW CAMP AT CLIPSTONE**

The people must have paid heed to this for although the Mansfield Brewery profits increased, no evidence has been found of alcohol causing exceptional concern. Drink however was only one concern of the Bishop. The other was women. He was aware of problems in other parts of the country where women in the company of soldiers, appeared to forget themselves, and 'dragged the men down.'[36] He placed the responsibility on the local community for the well being of everyone.

A month later the Bishop of Southwell extended this message. He said that families with young children should be on their guard, as children could easily overact and be unaware of the danger with soldiers. Young girls were of special concern and he suggested that they should be made aware of the potential dangers.[37] Rev. Wolfenden, senior curate at Grantham Parish Church spoke at a public meeting in Mansfield, and related the experiences at Grantham, where the Belton Camp was established. Once again the concern regarding the moral safety of young girls was expressed,

**'Parents should not let young girls parade the town after dark and bad women should not be allowed to come or remain in the town'.**[38]

To address the problems that arose in Grantham a women's police force was established. This became the nucleus of the nationwide women's police force.[39] Mansfield did not go to these extremes but ladies groups did organise Girls Clubs in an attempt the look after their welfare.

The warnings of the Church Leaders were heeded, because only a minority of cases appeared before the magistrates at the petty sessions. There were those however like Lucy Green, who chose to forget she was not allowed within ten miles of the camp.[40] Mary Hunt who 'was known for her style of living'[41] was discovered drunk with a crowd of soldiers in Mansfield.

Children were found wandering in and around the camp. One young boy was found there, trying to find his brother, a soldier stationed at the camp. This reflects the loss and insecurity of young children left behind when the older male members of a family left to participate in the war.

A number of long term relationships developed because of the camp. Marriages have been found taking place in churches in Mansfield, Mansfield Woodhouse, Edwinstowe, and Warsop where the groom's address is given as Clipstone Camp. Not all developed from friendships with local girls, the example below  from Edwinstowe Parish Registers reveal both bride and groom were stationed at Clipstone Camp.

| Percy Grewcock | Soldier | Clipstone Camp |
|---|---|---|
| Annie Marion Cockcroft | WAAC | Clipstone Camp |

| Walter Brookes | Soldier | Clipstone Camp |
|---|---|---|
| Eva Winifred Lock | WAAC | Clipstone Camp |

Both these marriages took place on the 12th December 1918

The two marriages above took place after banns which is done over a period of at least three weeks. Many of the other soldiers marriages discovered took place after a marriage licence had been obtained. This could have been for various reasons, the soldier may have been going away, or a girl had found she was pregnant. Not all girls were fortunate to get married and some illegitimate births did occur, but no evidence has been found that this was a major concern in the area. The report of the Medical Officer of Health in December 1917 lists 45 illegitimate births as opposed to

51 the previous year. How this compares to the years prior to building of Clipstone Camp is unknown.

No official figures have been discovered of the total number of soldiers that came to Clipstone Camp. Reports vary from 20,000 to 30,000 at any one time and possibly even more. What is known is that the presence of soldiers was everywhere and the camp and the community combined in many activities such as sport, religion and even death. The concern with morality, while never becoming a dominant issue, was nevertheless an important one. As the local economy expanded and the spending power of the soldiers and the camp took hold, the strong influence of the camp on the whole is easily recognised. Other issues did take place in Mansfield during the years of the Great War, Clipstone Camp, however, was a very influential element in the life of the community.

# END NOTES

1   Mansfield Reporter      27 Nov. 1914
2   Mansfield Chronicle     19 Nov. 1914
3   Mansfield Reporter       4 Dec. 1914
4   *The War Graves Of The British Empire, Cemeteries and Churchyards in Nottinghamshire,*(1930) pp. 26-27.
5   St Alban's Burial Register. Photocopy in Private Collection, the original has been deposited in NA.
6   Oral Histories, John Newton, Mrs Staley.
7   Chronicle Advertiser      6 Jul. 1917
8   Ripon Gazette            10 Nov. 1989   Article sent with personal correspondence from Ripon Library, North Yorkshire.
9   Personal correspondence with G H Flemming, 26 May 1997.
10  Mansfield Chronicle    27 June 1915  p. 1 col. 1-3
11     ibid.                27 Jun. 1915  p. 1 col. 1-3.
12     ibid.                17 May 1917  p. 8 col. 6.
13     ibid.                15 July 1915.
14     ibid.                5 Aug. 1915.
15  P.Bristow, *The Mansfield Brew,* (Ringwood Hants. 1976)p 76.
16  Mansfield Chronicle       1 Jun. 1916
17  Oral Histories, Mrs Staley, Rhoda Cope, Ken Nicholson.
18  Oral Histories, Mrs Staley, Rhoda Cope.
19  NUMD. Ma 2c 148/19/102
20     ibid. Ma 2c 148/19/85 & Ma 2c 148/19/137
21  This was, and still is a medium size lake now known as Vicar Water.
22  Mansfield Chronicle    10 Jun. 1915  p. 1 col. 5.
23  NA DC/M 1/1/24         7 Jun. 1915
24  Mansfield Chronicle    10 Jun. 1915  p. 8 col 1
25     ibid.                8 Jul. 1915  p. 5 col. 5.
26     ibid.                5 Aug. 1915
27  Stevenson & Woodward, *The First Hundred Years* (Notts 1995) p. 13
28  Brunts School Magazine Vol.1 No.10. 1917 p. 27 & No.12. pp 28-9.
29     ibid.                         Vol.I No II. 1918 pp. 1-2.
30  Mansfield Chronicle    15 Jun. 1916
31     ibid.                1 Aug. 1918
32     ibid.                9 Aug. 1918
33     ibid.                9 Aug. 1918
34     ibid.               22 Mar. 1917
35  Mansfield Reporter      4 Dec. 1914  p. 5 col. 3.
36     ibid.                1 Jan 1915  p. 3 col. 4.
37     ibid.                1 Jan.1915  p. 3 col. 4.
38     ibid.               15 Jan.1915  p. 3 col. 1-3.
39  M.Honeybone, *Book of Grantham, The History of a Market and Manufacturing Town,* (Buckingham 1980) p 103.
40  Mansfield Chronicle    20 Sep.1917  p. 8. col.5.
41     ibid.               22 Feb.1917  p. 1. col. 2.

# MANSFIELD AND THE REACTION TO WAR

BIG RALLY TO THE COLOURS

THE WAR
Four Questions
to Employers

MANSFIELD TRADE
AND THE WAR

SPECIAL TRAIN
ARRANGEMENTS FOR
TROOPS

THE MILITARY CAMP
AT MANSFIELD

PREPARATIONS AT
THE MANSFIELD
HOSPITAL

MUNITIONS WORK
BUREAU
Enrolment for War
Munitions Volunteers

# 6 - MANSFIELD AND THE REACTION TO WAR

While recruitment and the establishing of a military camp were significant to the Mansfield area during the years 1914-18, they were not the only issues of concern during that time. It is important to recognise that the Great War did have a wider influence on the locality and the local communities. Commercial enterprises, industry, and the environment were affected. Belgian refugees and wounded soldiers came to the area. People and the schools became involved in working for the war effort, the community were united in patriotic events, and celebrations. Additionally they were united in tragedies and deaths. They were all part of the consequences of war that placed additional demands on both the population and the locality.

In June 1913 Mansfield was recorded as being 'a busy thriving town with 40,000 inhabitants'. A large proportion of the working population were employed in established industries, such as the manufacture of textiles and shoes, iron foundries, tin box making, and brewing.[1] Coal mining was another major industry employing men and boys in the area. Mansfield was well connected to the outlying villages by a system of electric tramways.[2] The town was also connected by rail to both the Great Central and the Midland Railways. The new Mansfield Railway was in the course of construction. The war directly or indirectly affected all sectors of commerce. Government controls, shortages of goods, reduced labour, and rising prices all contributed to this.

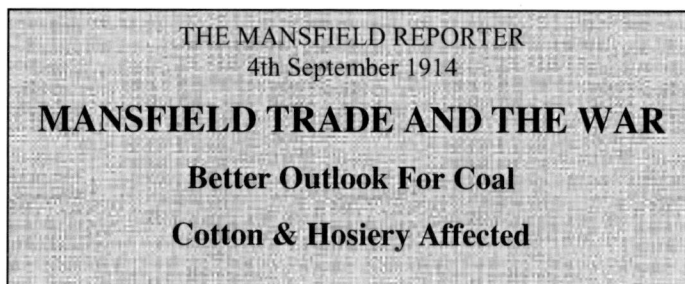

---

THE MANSFIELD REPORTER
4th September 1914

## MANSFIELD TRADE AND THE WAR

### Better Outlook For Coal

### Cotton & Hosiery Affected

---

In September 1914, trade was being affected, due to the restriction of overseas trading. Employees at the cotton doubling mills were on half time. Short time working had taken place at tin box manufactures in Mansfield, but this was improved by government contracts for shell casings, ammunition boxes and other military objects.[3] For the tin box industry the war was not only hectic, but profitable.

A shortage of wagons and the closing of sea routes for overseas exports had affected the local coal industry. However, Mansfield Colliery reported they were now better equipped with wagons and, once the Navy had cleared the seas of enemy ships, could export coal to Sweden and Norway.

The Mansfield shoe industry had orders from Germany and Austria cancelled, but still had sufficient work to employ their 400 workers. It also anticipated that orders to make boots would be received from the Government. Material was still obtainable to keep the local foundries running although costs had risen. One foundry became involved in producing bullets.[4] While in general most local industries were able to maintain a reasonable degree of business, one, a manure manufacturer went bankrupt. He attributed the blame to a shortage of horses caused by the war.[5]

A civil engineering development was already in progress when the war started. This was the new Mansfield Railway. The railway was only eleven miles long but it would be an important asset to the expansion of the coal mining industry, and the growth of Mansfield. Once completed the railway would provide the undeveloped coalfields with direct access to Immingham Docks. The route to London and Grimsby would be cut and the passenger services would be enhanced. The linking of this railway to the Great Central line, would be advantageous and profitable to both companies. In providing a feeder line to Immingham Docks local Colliery Companies would benefit, none more so than the Bolsover Colliery Company.

**John Plowright Houfton**

Mansfield Colliery, had in 1913 an output of 1.5 million tons per annum, 500,000 tons were expected to go for shipment at Immingham or Grimsby. When it was operational the Bolsover Colliery Company's new coal mine at Clipstone would be served entirely by the new railway. This was expected to produce a further 1 million tons per annum. The first section of the line between Mansfield and Clipstone Colliery opened for mineral traffic in June 1913. At a luncheon to mark the occasion it was said that the railway had a great future. The new enterprise had far reaching prospects not only for the development of the coalfields but for the future prosperity of Mansfield. J P Houfton, who made the statement was Chairman of the Railway, Director of Bolsover Colliery Company, and the present Mayor of Mansfield.[6] He had much to gain.

In August 1914, at the annual meeting of proprietors of the railway, J P Houfton presided and told the meeting of the continued progress of the line. The contracts were let for the building of a warehouse, and stations at Mansfield, Sutton-in-Ashfield and Kirkby-in-Ashfield. It was anticipated that, 'in the absence of unforeseen troubles the line would be completed by the end of March for mineral and goods traffic and about six months later for passenger traffic'.[7] However unforeseen troubles were on the horizon, and the outbreak of war inevitably delayed the completion of the railway.

When the passenger service finally opened in April 1917, the railway was not completely operational. Increased expenditure, plus a shortage of manpower and materials were contributory factors, all of which were accountable to the war. Lifts for the Mansfield Station 'had to be obtained from America owing to the pressure of Government work'.[8] Communications had been entered into with the Government for compensation during the period of Government control. This was made more complicated as they did not fall into the compensation category agreed between established railways and the government.[9]

A connection to the Clipstone Camp from the Clipstone Colliery branch line had involved discussions with both the military authorities and the Great Central Company.[10] It was October 1917 before a passenger service to the camp was finally in operation for the soldiers.[11] This was six months after the opening of the normal passenger service in Mansfield, an occasion that was done without great ceremony because of the wartime conditions. J P Houfton estimated that if it had not been for the war, the Railway would have been completed within both its budget and schedule, and they would have been running 20 trains a day not five.[12] He praised the contractors who had never asked for the exemption of a man that could not be spared from the war. He emphasised how the new shortened route between South Wales and Immingham, had been beneficial to the war in facilitating the transit of munitions to soldiers at the front.[13]

The new Mansfield Railway should have been beneficial to the local coal industry, instead the opening out of the coalfields and the urban expansion of Mansfield were disrupted by the war. The difficulty of obtaining materials and the shortage of skilled labour made it difficult to initiate large-scale development projects.[14] The new Clipstone Colliery and its associated village were early casualties and it was 1920 before sinking resumed there. At the outbreak of war coal mining was the dominant industry of the area. In Mansfield alone 43 per cent of the male workforce were employed in coal mining.[15]

Nationally, coal miners were encouraged to leave the industry and enlist for the war. The Bolsover Colliery Company for whom many Mansfield miners worked, claimed they had encouraged more men to enlist than any other colliery in the country. At the outbreak of war, 7,000 men were in their employment, now 2,000 had joined the army.[16] In March 1917, the company admitted it was paying the penalty as coal output was down. The greatest producers of coal had been the youngest and fittest men, they were now in the army and were not easy to replace.[17] Local newspapers carried many photos of soldiers who were listed as formerly being employed by Mansfield Colliery.

Historian A R Griffin discussing the national situation of miners who had voluntarily joined the Armed Forces, was also of the opinion that they were the 'pick of the manpower of the mining industry'.[18] He considered that replacements attracted to the industry were inexperienced and therefore production fell considerably.

An additional problem that beset the mining industry during the war was obtaining supplies of materials. Home produced goods were in short supply due to wartime conditions. This resulted in considerable price increases. A large proportion of timber for pit wood was imported before the war. The escalating cost and uncertainty of obtaining supplies resulted in the Government establishing a 'Central Joint Committee to organise the purchase and distribution of home grown timber'.[19] This shortage of timber effectively led to the founding of the Forestry Commission to ensure future supplies.[20]

The felling of trees to be used as pit props changed the landscape. The Mansfield Chronicle in December 1917, revealed that the 'picturesque spot near 'The Hut' on the Nottingham Road, was bleak, blackened and unlovely in appearance as the trees had been removed to be used as pit props'.[21] In other areas, trees that were straight and useful were doomed and Canadian Lumber Jacks arriving in the area were expected to stay a long time.[22] The writer declared 'it was better to sacrifice sylvan beauty for the freedom of the human race'.[23]

It was for the freedom of the human race that men were fighting. Many Belgian people had fled their country and became dependant on the hospitality of others. Shiploads of the refugees arrived at Folkestone with all their worldly possessions in a pocket-handkerchief.[24] Around a thousand refugees were found temporary accommodation at Alexander Palace, London, and from there the first family was selected to come to Mansfield. Local newspaper headlines read:-

**BELGIAN REFUGEES**

**ARRIVAL AT MANSFIELD**

**THEIR NEW HOME AT MANSFIELD**

(9th October 1914)

**GRATEFUL BELGIANS**

**MANSFIELD'S HOSPITALITY TO THE REFUGEES**

(16th October 1914)

**MORE BELGIANS**
**AT MANSFIELD**

**ARRIVAL OF ANOTHER BIG PARTY**

(23rd October 1914)

In October 1914 Madam Von Avond with her six children and their 62 year old grandfather, Frans de Vodder, arrived at Mansfield Station, where a small group of the more affluent members of the town greeted them. Among them was Mr J W Houfton[25] who had provided a furnished house for the family at Ollerton, ten-miles from Mansfield.[26]

Within days more refugees were arriving in the town. They came from all levels of the Belgian society: a judge from Charloeroi, a merchant from Genappe, and others who were less fortunate. Curiosity and genuine concern for the welfare of the Belgian people encouraged large crowds of Mansfield people to turn out and greet them at the station.

Accommodation was found for the refugees in Mansfield, Mansfield Woodhouse, and Bolsover, Derbyshire. The finding and preparing accommodation for the refugees involved people from all social classes of the local society. Donations were received from many people including Countess Manvers of Thoresby Hall, she provided furniture and food. A girl at the Hermitage Mill, Mansfield, made and sold cloth iron holders, raising funds of fourteen shillings.[27] There were many others. The arrival of the Belgian refugees brought home the personal consequences of war to the people of the Mansfield area. They were enthusiastic in their help.

**Mansfield Reporter 23rd October 1914**

**COUNTESS MANVERS**
AND
**REFUGEES**
**NEAR MANSFIELD**

**DELEGATES MEETING**

The reception and welfare of wounded soldiers became an early priority in Mansfield. Though Lincoln was the Territorial Base Hospital for the district and would receive the first wounded, Mansfield, in anticipation made its own preparations. Members of the local Red Cross Society prepared a ward in the Mansfield Hospital to accommodate the wounded. In addition, the hospital authorities placed other wards and beds at the disposal of the Red Cross. The Red Cross nurses would staff the relevant wards.

Additional preparations were made to take care of soldiers who needed convalescence. An appeal by the Red Cross resulted in the offer of accommodation from all over Nottinghamshire. The private residences of Welbeck Abbey, Sherwood Lodge, and Teversal Manor were included. Each home was to be staffed by voluntary aid detachments working under trained nurses. A list of suitable vehicles was compiled to transport the wounded from railway stations.[28]

Mansfield Hospital

The preparations were justified. In March 1915, twenty-two wounded soldiers were patients in the Mansfield Hospital and Mr R H King the Hon Secretary to the Red Cross Society, appealed for:-

> 'games such as cards, dominoes, draughts, books, periodicals, gramophone records and anything to contribute to the amusement or entertainment of the wounded men would be gratefully received by the Matron or himself. There are a number of men who are unable to walk, and offers of motor-cars for drives in the afternoon will be very acceptable.'[29]

On the 21st May 1915 The Mansfield Reporter carried the headline,

## PATIENTS FROM THE FRONT
### Mansfield Hospital Nearly Full

'There were now 45 men in hospital and the available beds number 50.' The newspaper listed the names, numbers and regiments of the 22 soldiers who had been sent on from Lincoln the previous Saturday. The local detachment of the Red Cross had assisted with transferring the men from the train to the hospital.

Over the next four years 20 per cent of the patients in the hospital were soldiers.

| YEAR | TOTAL PATIENTS | SOLDIERS | % SOLDIERS |
|---|---|---|---|
| 1915 | 954 | 152 | 16% |
| 1916 | 1178 | 392 | 33% |
| 1917 | 1076 | 147 | 14% |
| 1918 | 1224 | 212 | 17% |
| TOTAL | 4432 | 903 | 20% |

**Compiled from the Annual Reports
of Mansfield and District Hospital**

The largest number admitted in 1916, coincides with the Battles of the Somme, and Jutland. No indication is given however, in surviving hospital records, of where the soldiers came from, or what type of wounds they had received. The increased workload of the hospital was made more difficult when members of the medical staff joined the colours. The use of a newly equipped ophthalmic department had to be suspended due to staff shortages.[30] Beds in the hospital were also allotted for soldiers from Clipstone Camp.

In the years before the National Health Service, hospitals were dependent on donations and subscriptions for their funding. The War Office agreed to the charge of three shilling a day for wounded soldiers in the hospital.[31] In 1918, the sum of £1581-4-0d was received for the treatment of 212 soldiers during that year. In that same year, the hospital also treated 43 soldiers on leave and 16 discharged soldiers.[32] Each year the hospital acknowledged the community help it received in caring for the soldiers:

*'The Board also desire to express their thanks to the Voluntary Aid Detachment of the Red Cross for the provision of Nurses for the Military Ward; to the various owners of motor cars for their assistance in transferring Wounded Soldiers from the Station to the Hospital; to the Management of the various places of amusement in the town for allowing the Wounded Soldier to attend performances at their respective Houses; and the Tramways Co. for allowing the Soldiers to use their cars free of charge.'[33]*

While the free transporting of wounded soldiers was done as a charitable gesture, it was a different scenario for the healthy soldiers of Clipstone Camp. The thousands of soldiers at the camp increased the use of public transport.[34] The local tramcar system terminated a few miles from the camp but was nevertheless well used.

Many soldiers just walked the four-mile from Mansfield to the camp or took advantage of a taxi. A taxi system in and around the Mansfield area developed rapidly because of the camp. Quick thinking entrepreneurs were soon applying to the local councils for driving or omnibus licences, while others were requesting a licence to store petrol. It was an offence to ply for hire near the camp without a licence and some people were convicted of this.[35]

Shadrach Osler seen on the left in the picture above was the Forest Town Postmaster and a car owner. He was quick to establish a taxi service and was recalled as having charge 6d a journey.[36] The taxis created additional use of the road between Mansfield and the camp. Increased road traffic resulted in a number of accidents, some fatal.

The railways were also swift to provide extra trains for the soldiers to go on leave. The local newspapers carried advertisements of the special trains available.

Mansfield Chronicle 8th July 1915
### Special Train Arrangements
### For Troops

Trains that left Mansfield (Midland) Station provided a link to the railway network that would take soldiers as far as Scotland or Ireland. In October 1917, the Mansfield Railway finally opened a passenger service to the camp. This not only reduced the traffic on the roads but also the income of the taxi drivers. For the Mansfield Railway Company, the number of passengers using the new service proved very profitable.[37]

Loss of trade due to war shortages does not seem apparent in Mansfield as Clipstone Camp was an asset to the commercial life of the town. Trade for local firms was good as they supplied the camp with big orders.[38]

Badley's clothing shop on Church Street made a decision to stock clothing required by soldiers and would even sew on a stripe for 2d a bar as this advert in July 1915 reveals.

How long they offered soldiers clothing is unknown. However they were obviously aiming to keep their trade with an emphasis on the war as a few months later at the end of October, their advert had changed. It is now headed 'Warfare Means War Fare' and they are offering reasonably priced boys clothing to help offset the high price of food. Amongst the clothes on offer are 'Odd knickers at low prices.'

Smaller firms like the Brameld Cycle Company charged 6d to deliver a parcel to the camp,[39] and local newsagents had paperboys delivering to the camp for them.[40]

**Badley's, Church St.**

PRICE LIST FOR SOLDIERS' REQUISITES.

Serge Jackets, 21/6, 25/-.
Do. Slacks, 13/6, 15/-.
Bedford Cord Breeches, 16/6, 25/-, 30/-
Service Caps, 3/11.
Khaki Shirts, 3/11.
Aertex Cellular Do., 5/-.
Aertex Vests and Pants, 3/-., 3/6, 4/-.
Worsted Socks, 6½d., 1/-, 1/3, 1/6, 1/11.
Cap Covers, 1/-. Protectors, 6½d.
Stripes, 2d. per bar, if sewn on jackets, 1d. extra.
Fox's Puttees, 5/6.
Handkerchiefs, 6½d.
Towels, 6½d., 8½d., 10½d., 1/-.

**Badley's, Church St.**

THE SHOP WHERE THE FLAG FLIES.

**WILLMAN,**
THE STATIONER
White Hart St., MANSFIELD
FOR CAMP
**STATIONERY**
WITH REGT. CREST
FOR
**Royal Fusiliers**
**King's Royal Rifles**
**Middlesex Regt.**
**Essex Regt.**
**Royal Engineers**
**A.S.C., &c.**

Printed camp stationery was offered on sale in many shops such as Willman's in White Hart Street, Mansfield.[41]

As the war continued at the end of November 1916 this shop also carried a small poignant advert.

**IN MEMORIAM CARDS**
In response to numerous requests from relatives of our fallen soldiers, we can now offer cards especially designed for the purpose. Samples may be seen at F Willman's, White Hart Street, or at the Works, Bridge Street.

Willman's Stationery shop in Mansfield set a room aside for soldiers to 'write their post cards without hindrance'.[42] The sending of cards and letters provided an important, and possibly the only means of communication between soldiers and their families. In the early months of the war (October 1914) eleven of Mansfield's Postmen had been called up, three indoor workers and four outdoor. At that time the postmaster did not see any problems as the men's places had been filled, however things were soon to change when Clipstone Camp was built.

In July 1916, the average daily despatch of letters and parcels from the camp was 3,100.[43] This compares to Witley Camp in Surrey with four YMCA huts, who despatched thousands of items daily.[44] The vast quantity of mail to and from Clipstone Camp radically increased the workload of the Post Office in Mansfield.[45]

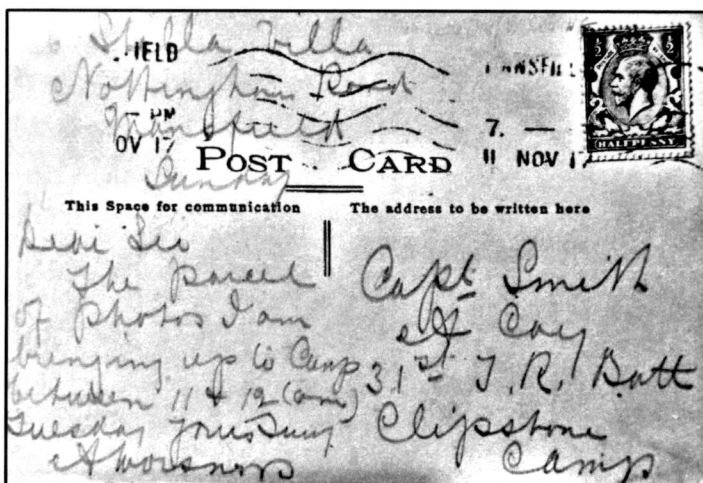

*Post card sent to*
**Captain Smith**
**A Coy**
**31st T R Batt.**
**Clipstone Camp**

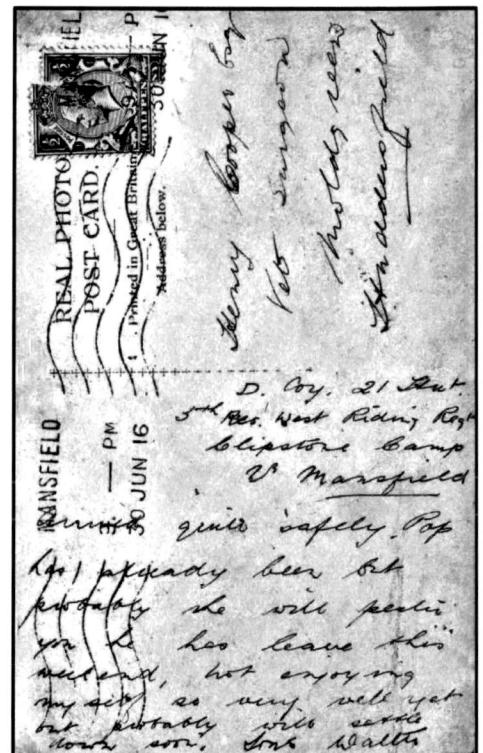

*Post card sent from*
**'Walter'**
**21 Hut**
**5th Res. West Riding Regt.**
**Clipstone Camp,**
**Nr Mansfield**

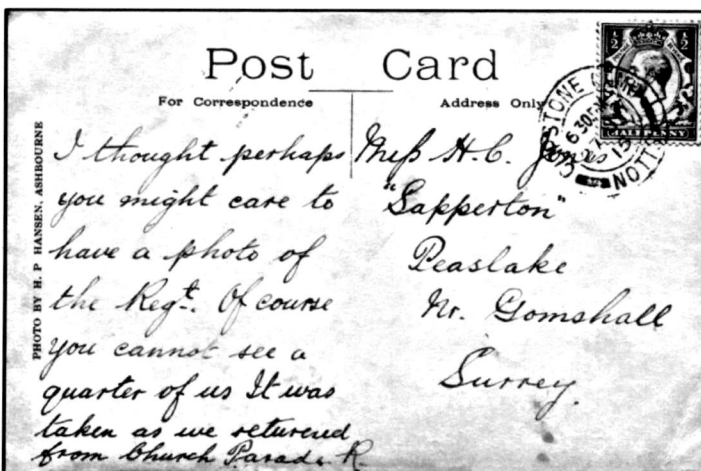

*Post Card with*
**'Clipstone Camp'**
*Postmark*

Soldiers did not just send pictures of Clipstone Camp, they also sent them of the locality. Messages would mention 'The coal mine gets up 30,000 tons of coal a day, it is one of the largest', - 'Just off down to Forest Town', - 'Just let you know what sort of a place this is' which told about the community they were residing in.

The public-spirited attitude of the community was apparent everywhere and schools were no exception. The children at St John's School, Mansfield brought seven dozen eggs as a contribution towards the national egg collection, which were sent to London. Money was raised to send Christmas gifts to soldiers at the front, while fruit and vegetables were sent to sailors. For the soldiers' huts at Clipstone Camp the children made paper flower decorations.[46] The value of food economy was stressed in the schools and lessons at St John's School included gardening in the Master's garden and in an allotment assigned to them by the Borough Surveyor.[47]

At Forest Town the school closed for half a day to enable the children to gather blackberries, 83½ pounds were picked.[48]

Sept 27th 18.

The school was closed yesterday (Thursday) afternoon so that the children might go blackberry picking. In the two half-days 83½ lbs have been picked.

Another local school during a short school holiday organised the gathering of horse chestnuts by older boys. The chestnuts were forwarded to the Director of Propellant Supplies, they were 'required to save grain in the making of high explosives'.[49]

Pupils at the Brunts Grammar School in Mansfield participated in many fund-raising activities and collections for the war effort. Woollen garments were knitted. Chocolate, cigarettes and OXO cubes were collected. Parcels were made and sent to the troops. The school had many former pupils serving in the war and they were proud of this.

In October 1914, the school magazine declared 'Let the Brunts School be able to put a Roll of Honour second to none in the Country'.[50] They were quick to record the names of former pupils who were on active service. Their exploits were followed throughout the war, and their injuries, awards, and deaths were noted. Among the heading 'Killed in Action' were:-

| | | |
|---|---|---|
| Lce-Corpl. R Hotson Sherwood Foresters | | 1915 |
| Pte J F Husskison R.F | | 1916 |
| Pte S Alvey (Killed in Egypt) | April | 1917 |
| QMS H Gadd. Sherwood Foresters | May | 1917 |
| Ord.Tel. H Roberts | Jan | 1918 |

The magazine was posted to soldiers, sailors and nurses who had once been pupils at the school. Maintaining contact with former scholars was an important school policy. Letters the school received from Egypt, Turkey, and France, gave an awareness of the distances previous school members had travelled because of the war. Others remained in England and were stationed at many camps including the one at Clipstone. An Army Cadet Corps at the school was established with assistance from officers at the Clipstone Camp. The forming of this Cadet Corps was considered 'as a tribute to the self sacrifice of 'Old Boys' who so nobly had responded to the call of duty'.[51]

The community united on many occasions and in the early months of the war a great deal was made of an outstanding award that was made to the son of a Mansfield miner, who had also previously worked at the Mansfield Colliery. This was Lance-Corporal W. D. Fuller of the Grenadier Guards, who was awarded the Victoria Cross in 1915 after a battle at Neuve Chapelle on March 12th.

## Mansfield Welcomes Her V.C. Hero.

### Lance-Corporal Fuller Decorated " For Valour."

### The Town's Appreciation.    Last Night's Presentations.

At the end of May 1915 a civic reception for Lance Corporal Fuller was held in Mansfield Market Place, it was heralded by the music of the Mansfield Colliery Band. People from surrounding villages joined the local inhabitants to pay homage to the V.C.

The presence of wounded soldiers from Mansfield hospital and soldiers from Clipstone Camp added to the military tributes.

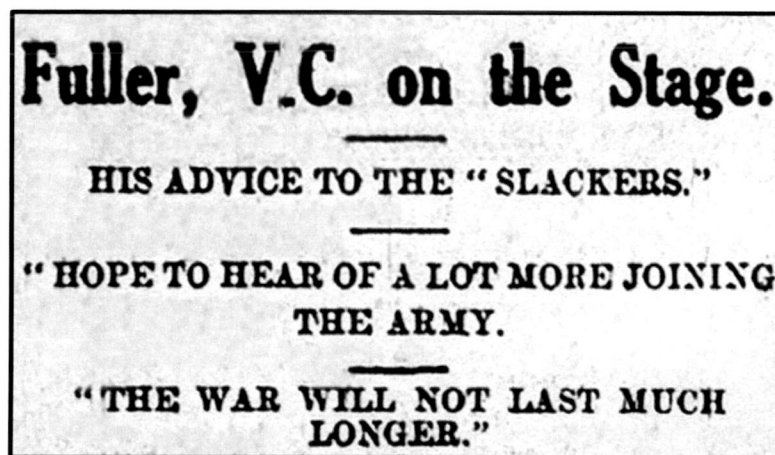

## Fuller, V.C. on the Stage.

### HIS ADVICE TO THE " SLACKERS."

### " HOPE TO HEAR OF A LOT MORE JOINING THE ARMY.

### "THE WAR WILL NOT LAST MUCH LONGER."

The occasion was used to emphasise and encourage the need for young single men to recruit and serve their country.[52] Lance-Corporal Fuller appeared in public on a number of occasions and stressed to others the value of being patriotic and bringing honour to the town.

In the early months of 1917 an invitation to join in a Patriotic Fair for the City and County of Nottingham was declined, instead Mansfield and the surrounding neighbourhoods decided to hold their own Patriotic Fair. The fair, which took place over two days in June, was held in the town's Titchfield Park with Mansfield, Clipstone Camp, and many local villages participating. Thirty one stallholders demonstrated the total commitment of the whole area. These included:

> Various Schools
> The Red Cross
> Hosiery Manufacturers
> The Stanton Ironworks Company
> Clipstone Camp
> Church Organisations
> Local Villages
> Mansfield Grocers

MANSFIELD & DISTRICT
PATRIOTIC FAIR.
THE FOLLOWING PLACES IN THE
Antient Forest of Sherwood
ARE PARTICIPATING IN THE EFFORT :—
MANSFIELD
PLEASLEY HILL
MANSFIELD WOODHOUSE
FOREST TOWN
CLIPSTONE CAMP
BLIDWORTH
RAINWORTH
WARSOP
EDWINSTOWE
LANGWITH
CUCKNEY
FARNSFIELD
SKEGBY
STANTON HILL
TEVERSAL
ANNESLEY

Titchfield Park, Mansfield,
FRIDAY & SATURDAY, 22ND & 23RD JUNE, 1917.

Other stalls included those organised by the Duchess of Portland, Lady Victoria Bentinck, and Lady Sealy. Cattle and gift auctions were an additional attraction and there was musical entertainment by the massed bands from Clipstone Camp. Other groups provided entertainment in the form of physical drill, dancing and concerts.[53]

Over 20,000 people attended the event on the 22nd - 23rd June 1917. The event was held to raise funds for local War Charities, and was not considered a festivity, but a tribute to those who had participated in the war.[54]

Stall at the Patriotic Fair held in Mansfield June 1917

In March 1918 there was once again a local event that encouraged people of all ages to congregate in Mansfield Market Place. This was worthy of an entry in St John's School Log Book:

> *March 7ᵗʰ 1918*
>
> *School was dismissed at 11.30 to enable the scholars to view the proceedings in the Market Place. A route march of over 5,000 troops from Clipstone Camp and a visit of a squadron of aeroplanes was the chief feature of this morning's programme.*

This event was about Mansfield raising sufficient money to purchase three submarines - a Boom Week effort. It is unknown if this was achieved but for the people of Mansfield and District this was just another aspect of their Great War.

# END NOTES

1   The Railway News 21 June 1913, p 1248 as found in, TNA: PRO RAIL 226/558.
2   ibid.
3   Mansfield Museum and Art Gallery, Temporary Exhibition August 1997.
4   Mansfield Reporter             4 Sep.1914   p. 8 col. 3
5   Mansfield Chronicle           21 Jun. 1917  p. 7 col. 2
6   The Railway News              21 Jun. 1913  p. 1251 as found in, TNA: PRO RAIL 226/558
7   Mansfield Reporter             7.Aug.1914   p. 5 col. 2
8   TNA: PRO RAIL 468/1 No 792 25 Oct.1916
9   The Railway News              21 April 1917  p (n.g.) as found in, TNA: PRO RAIL 226/558
10  TNA: PRO RAIL 468/1 No 794 25 Oct.1916
11  Mansfield Chronicle           4 Oct.1917   p. 5 col. 1
12     ibid.                      5 April 1917  p. 1 col. 1-3
13     ibid.
14  A R Griffin, *Mining in the East Midlands, 1550-1947* (1971), p 171.
15  D Crute, 'The Industrial Development of Mansfield Since 1891', in [n.g.]*Mansfield: The Last Century* (Nottingham 1991), pp.82-89.
16  Mansfield Chronicle           8 Mar. 1917  p. 5 col. 2
17     ibid.                      8 Mar. 1917  p. 5 col. 2
18  A R Griffin  *Mining in the East Midlands, 1550-1947* (1971),p 171.
19     ibid.                         p 173.
20  A J P Taylor, *English History 1914-1945,* (Oxford 1965), p 84.
21  Mansfield Chronicle           6 Jan.1917   p. 5 col. 2.
22     ibid.                     21 Jun. 1918  p. 2 col. 3 baseball match between  teams at the Canadian Forestry Corps. stationed at Mansfield and Worksop.
23  Mansfield Chronicle           6 Jan.1917   p. 5 col. 2
24  Mansfield Reporter            9 Oct.1914   p. 3 col. 1-2
25  Brother of John P. Houfton
26  Mansfield Reporter            9 Oct.1914   p. 3 col. 1-2
27     ibid.                     16 Oct.1914   p. 3 col. 1-2
28     ibid.                      4 Sep.1914   p. 8 col. 3.
29     ibid.                     19 Mar. 1915  p. 5
30  Mansfield & District Hospital Annual Report  31 Dec. 1915.
31  Mansfield & District Hospital Minute Book      1909 -1920.
32  Mansfield & District Hospital Annual Report  31 Dec. 1918.
33     ibid.                     31 Dec. 1918
34  Mansfield Chronicle           8 Jul.1915   p. 2 col. 4
35  NA. DC/M 1/1/25              5 Jan.1917
36  Oral History Derek Osler     3 Feb. 1994
37  TNA: PRO RAIL 468/11
38  Mansfield Reporter           21 May 1915  p. 8 col. 3
39  Mansfield Chronicle           2 May 1918  p. 4 col. 1
40  Oral History, Mrs Storey.
41  Mansfield Chronicle          15 May 1915  p. 2 col. 4
42     ibid.                      8 Jul.1915   p. 2 col. 4
43     ibid.                     13 Jul.1916   p. 2. col. 6
44  Surrey Advertiser            21 Aug.1915  Article sent from Surrey Local Studies Library.
45  NA. DC/MW 1/3/5/4           26 Jul 1915
46  J. Noble, *Extracts from St John's School Log Book 1859-1950.*
47     ibid.
48  Forest Town School Log Book, Mixed Department 1914-18.
49  J, Noble, *Extracts from St Johns School Log Book 1859-1950.*
50  Brunts School Magazine, Vol. 1 No 3. 1914.
51     ibid.              Vol. II No 1.1918.
52  Mansfield Chronicle          10 Jun. 1915  p. 2 col. 1-6
53  Patriotic Fair Programme     Jun. 1917
54     ibid.                     Jun. 1917

# 7 - THE LOCAL WOMEN'S WAR

A great deal has been written about the role of women during the First World War, suggesting that this was a watershed in the lives of the female population. Women had been struggling for recognition in society for many years and only a minority had succeeded. Collectively their strength and ability was not recognised or accepted by their male counterparts, women were seen as a threat to the male orientated work place.

In 1914 the majority of the female working population was employed in industry and domestic service. Only 542,000 were placed in the category of professional workers, these included nurses, secretaries and typists.

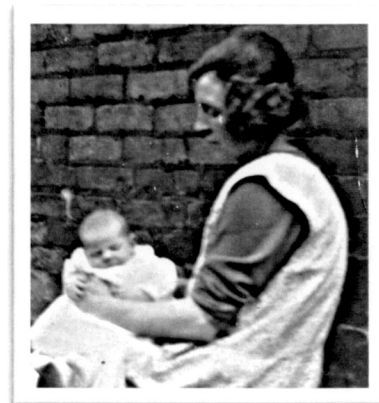

The greatest proportion of women were occupied in the home as a wife, mother or widowed dependant.[1] 'In general the respectable British working man preferred his wife not to work outside the home.'[2] Her place was with the children.

It was an attitude that was difficult to sustain as the demands of the war drained Britain of its male working population. The general running of the country had to be maintained. The military armies were in need of constant supplies, placing new and greater demands on industry. Nurses were needed to care for the wounded and the welfare and morale of the soldiers became a significant issue.

New considerations were given to the necessary employment of female labour culminating in a wide belief that a great many women participated in the national effort. While historians Bourne and Marwick do not dispute women's contribution to the war, they both suggest that it is easy to select local facts and create an impressive national picture.[3] To what extent women in the Mansfield locality fitted into the national picture will be discovered in this chapter.

The opportunities to participate in paid or voluntary employment, were determined by many individual elements which were all relevant features:-

> The environment and type of community
> Local occupations and industry
> Social class
> The driving force of people in the locality

In close proximity to Mansfield were a number of country estates such as Welbeck Abbey, (Duke of Portland), and Thoresby (Earl Manvers). Such estates encompassed forest, heathland, and a large proportion of agricultural land, providing work for labourers and tenant farmers. Newly sunk coal mines provided work for men and boys but nothing for the female population of the new mining communities.

In 1911, the male and female population of the Mansfield Borough were of a similar proportion[4] to the national figure for England and Wales.[5] Of the female population in Mansfield 21.7 per cent were employed, this was below the national average of 25.9 per cent.[6]

The Mansfield Reporter in September 1914 reassured its readers about the effect of war on local trade. It considered local people, of whom a proportion were females, would be kept in employment.[7]

In December 1914 the Annual Report on sanitary and social conditions for Mansfield confirmed that a good deal of female labour was employed in hosiery, cotton, and tin box works, adding that only a minority continued to work after marriage.[8] No further indication is given on the state of female employment in future council minutes.

A lack of further newspaper reports on the local industries suggests that employment was maintained throughout the war. No evidence has been found to the contrary. If a shortage of manpower in the mills and factories did occur, because of military recruitment, it does not appear to have been a major concern within the town. The 1911 census figures indicate there was a surplus of female labour should this be required.

Certain essential services of the town did have to depend on the assistance of women. The Mansfield Council Minutes of December 1914 include a report of the Gas Committee:

'Slot Meter Collectors enlisted, women employed'.[9]

The report suggested females were only employed out of necessity. Both respect and concern was shown for women in 1915 when they were employed on the Mansfield and District Light Railway. The General Purposes Committee requested the Council place notices in the tramcars warning against the use of offensive language. A further suggestion was made that women were not employed as conductors on the workmen's cars.[10]

The recognition of female status was only partly adhered to by the Local Health Committee when they required a temporary replacement for Doctor Lambie who was serving with His Majesty's Forces. The salary was to be £400.

> Qualified ladies are invited to apply
> for vacant positions
> of
> 'Medical Officer of Health
> and
> School Medical Officer'
> at a salary
> of £500 per annum.

The British Medical Journal and the Lancet refused the request to place the advertisement in their journals, as the recognised minimum salary for the two combined posts should be £500. The Council accepted the importance of filling this vacancy and agreed to the new salary.[11]

Only a minimum of evidence has been found of local women moving away to participate in war related occupations. The Red House at Loughborough, formerly a college was used by the Ministry of Munitions during the war as a women's hostel. They ran a variety of courses in munitions engineering from where the girls would go to work in various munitions factories.

Norah Brooks a 20 year old Mansfield mill girl trained at the Red House during 1916. Afterwards she worked in the Tail Plane and Elevation Department of William Lawrence & Co. Ltd, Colwick, Nottingham.[12] No records of girls residing and training at Loughborough have survived so it is unknown how many other girls from the Mansfield area went there. It can be assumed that others did go at that time, as it would be rather unusual for one girl from a factory environment to have taken such an initiative to leave home on her own.

The local newspapers of October 1916[13] make reference to women working in munitions. The Duke of Portland lecturing on the war in March 1917 considered that 'two classes more than any others are helping to save the country, miners and women in munitions factories'.[14] Mr J. P. Houfton also spoke of the great many women who had left their homes in Mansfield to work in munitions.[15]

Of all those women the names of only two have been discovered: Norah Brooks the local mill girl and the Duke of Portland's own daughter, who received local acknowledgement for her participation in munitions work.

**'Lady Victoria Bentinck, daughter of the Duke of Portland
is doing a full day's work and taking meals with other
factory hands in an aeroplane munitions factory in the
London District'.[16]**

The Duke of Portland also advocated the work of women on the land and he authorised a centre for training women at Welbeck in 1916.[17] Additionally it was planned to open a centre at Colston Bassett, and both places were to be run by the Nottinghamshire Education Committee.

The need for women to work on the land was often a feature in the local newspapers, however very few women worked in an agricultural capacity around the Mansfield area.

Mansfield Chronicle 11th May 1916

**Appeal to Mansfield Women
To work as Individuals
or in squads**

The organiser of labour for the Board of Agriculture spoke to a meeting in Mansfield during August 1917. She told of the women workers from Nottingham University College who were now working at Ollerton, singling turnips, spudding(sic) etc. doing excellent work. She had additional groups of women available who was anxious to get into the area, the rate of pay was 4[d] per hour for a 10 hour day and 5[d] per hour for any overtime.[18] Farmers in the district appeared reluctant to use female labour which is not surprising when at times they had been fortunate to obtain soldiers on temporary release from their military duties.[19]

By October 1917 it was felt the time was drawing near when there was less demand for women working on the land and it was decided to close the Centre at Welbeck. Thus this local training opportunity for women drew to a close.[20]

For some women the nursing of the wounded became their vocation during the Great War. The Matron of the Mansfield Hospital, Miss Balydon moved away to serve for five years in the 4th Northern Hospital at Lincoln. She was decorated in 1917 with the Royal Red Cross (1st Class) for her services during the war.[21] During her absence various temporary matrons were in charge of the nursing staff, Miss M Mason (1915), Miss E E Jones (1917), Miss E J Mildred (1918). It was 1919 when Miss Balydon resumed her duties at the Mansfield Hospital. [22]

MANSFIELD HOSPITAL.                                                                          G.9845.

At the Mansfield Hospital, 25 beds were allocated for use by the military authorities, and extra nursing assistance was required for the duration of the war to care for the wounded soldiers. This continued until December 1918.

Members of the Voluntary Aid Detachment provided nurses for the military ward from Mansfield, and the surrounding villages. They worked under a trained sister.[23] The Commandant of the British Red Cross Society reported on the work of the Mansfield Detachment for 1916. She spoke of the members who worked in Mansfield Hospital and the Military Hospital at Clipstone Camp. When the Voluntary Aid Detachments (VAD) were formed in 1910, they were allowed to include both men and women. However, Marwick (Historian) maintains that as the main work of the organisation was in the field of nursing, most of the recruits were women.[24] No evidence has been found to contradict this. The work of the V.A.D. was voluntary and unpaid but this did not deter women from around the Mansfield area.

Members who were free to leave home left to work in Military hospitals in Birmingham, Woolwich, France, Malta, and Belgium.[25] Professional nursing was undertaken by former female pupils of the Brunt's Grammar School, Nurse Norah Hammond one of Queen Alexandra's Imperial Military Nurses in France was a regular correspondent to the school. Both she and two other 'old girls' Nurse Pearce (Salonika,) and Nurse Willies (Alexandria), appear in the list of over 350 names in the School Roll of Honour. The rest are 'old boys' who were serving in the army and navy.[26]

For many women, (and men) there was no Roll of Honour on which their names were inscribed but their contribution to the war effort was of equal importance. They were the volunteers who put in hours of work in a variety of different ways for the comfort and social welfare of soldiers and sailors, and the people at home.

Nationally many different associations were established. Locally it was left to the ability of individual people to organise. People who had both the knowledge and the contacts to co-ordinate various projects and encourage the involvement of members of the community. It was an area where the women of a higher social standing could participate while their male counterparts were active with the recruiting campaigns for military enlistment. The Duchess of Portland, Lady Victoria Bentinck and Violet Markham were often to be found chairing meetings and making speeches. There were other less well known leaders such as Mrs Bainbridge, the Houfton ladies and Mrs Stacey, wives and daughters of local business men and councillors who were all to be found organising or helping with a variety of activities.

In April 1915, Lady Victoria Bentinck presided over a mass meeting for women and girls held in the YMCA Hall in Mansfield. Those present were advised of the many ways at which they could help their country during the war.[27] One of her own initiatives was the establishing of a War Hospital Depot in Mansfield. On the first anniversary of the Mansfield Branch, she gave thanks to the people of the whole area for their contributions and help in making 48,860 articles. Among the articles were towels, pillows, bed rests, crutches, splints, and bandages.[28]

The Mansfield Red Cross Voluntary Aid Detachment who have been mentioned previously for their nursing skills had two emergency dressing stations ready in the town, should an air raid occur. In addition they had sewing parties established in the surrounding villages where members made garments such as pyjamas, shirts, socks, mufflers, helmets and mittens. This resulted in parcels of clothes being sent to fighting men and prisoners of war.[29]

In July 1915 Mansfield ladies received a royal acknowledgement which was reported in the Mansfield Chronicle 8th July 1915.

*'Queen Alexandra has sent to the women of Mansfield Emergency Corps, who have a shop in White Hart Street her sincere thanks for their contribution of a number of cushions 12inch square, for the use of wounded soldiers at the casualty clearing stations at the front. The useful gift was made to Her Majesty's Field Force Fund, and in her acknowledgement the secretary, Mrs Charlotte Slater writes;- these cushions are a great boon to invalids with wounds. Please convey to the women our grateful thanks.'*

The newspaper revealed more of the work the women were doing and how it benefited the war effort.

*'Now the workers are engaged in making a consignment of bags which will go to France and the Dardinelles and will be used for keeping together the contents of the pockets of the sick and wounded which would otherwise get lost. The bags are of calico and a piece of white linen is sewn on for the soldiers name, regiment and number. There is no waste in this workroom, for all the cushions which have been sent out are stuffed with the odd pieces of material after cutting out. A number of arm rests have also been made and have been sent to the Mansfield Hospital for use by the wounded men.*

*There are now about two dozen women on the books at White Hart Street depot, ten of them being toy makers, they have taken to the making of toys extremely well, and some clever work is being done. There has been a good demand for the articles made, the Duchess of Portland being among the purchasers. One of the girls is quite adept at cutting out the figures of men, women and animals in wood, and several Mansfield ladies give their services in sketching and painting the feature and dress on the models.'*

Local women also worked at the 'Tin Box Factory' (Barringer Wallis & Manners Ltd) and would have been present when Her Grace the Duchess of Portland and Lady Victoria Cavendish-Bentinck paid a private visit to the works in December 1914. They had gone to see special brass boxes being manufactured for the troops, known as Princess Mary's Boxes, and were specially interested in the embossing of the design on the lid bearing a medallion of the Princess Mary.[30]

Many local women were involved with providing refreshments for the soldiers from Clipstone Camp. They worked either at the camp or in the town or surrounding villages where facilities were often provided by religious establishments. For the churches, chapels and the Salvation Army who provided these facilities it could incur extra essential requirements and expense.

The Forest Town Church Mission had to apply for a supply of water, 'the water to be used for providing tea, coffee etc. for entertaining soldiers from Clipstone Camp'.[31] An application granted for that purpose was charged at the nominal rate of one shilling per year.

Forest Town Mission
next to St Alban's Church

Organisations like the Wesleyan Methodists paid tribute to their workers by presenting them with war badges, 140 helpers at the Bridge Street Church received these in July 1918. The 'Wesleyan Rest' specific rooms for soldiers recreation had opened in 1915. They were managed by a committee of ladies who provided refreshments and social activities for soldiers from the camp. In three years, they catered for over a million men.[32]

Bridge Street Church

Catering was also a major function of the YMCA whose emblem was a Red Triangle. They had large premises on Church Lane in Mansfield. In January 1915 it was arranged that these rooms would provide welfare facilities for the troops coming to Clipstone Camp. Additional three huts were established at the camp for the same purpose.[33] These were placed under the supervision of male leaders such as Mr F Peel, the leader of No 3 Hut,[34] and at least twelve ladies under the guidance of a Miss Birks, travelled daily to work voluntarily in

YMCA Church Lane

the YMCA huts at the camp.[35] The work there involved serving refreshments, and serving behind the counters of the shop and Post Office. The vast quantity of mail sent from the camp was an indication of how the various enterprises were used and the amount of work involved.

An orderly stationed at the camp, wrote of 'the pleasant smiles and loving devotion of the ladies who gave so much of their time',[36] while another appreciation, naming some of the Mansfield helpers was written in the autograph book of Lily Chadwick:-

### The Mansfield YMCA Staff

There's a hearty place of welcome which you can easily find
And the lasses who look after you are so jolly and so kind.

There's Nora always smiling and Lily what a nut,
There's Mrs Harvey such a dear, she could not say tut-tut.

There's Mrs Chadwick we call Mother,
we are sure she will not mind,
Because to us she is like those, that we have left behind.

But then there are the others, we must not leave them out,
Because to us they are so kind, we have not the slightest doubt.

There's Mrs Mee & Mrs Ward, both helping like the rest,
And then there's Nellie Redfern, just trying to do her best.

There's Edith too and Mrs Hall,
who have answered the call that's true,

And mean to stick to their hard work,
and see the whole thing through.

So we will close and wish them luck,
Good health and happiness too,

And proud to say they have done their bit,
for the lads in Khaki & Blue.

*Pte G H Ward  MGC Clipstone 25 Nov 1917*

The picture below shows many of the ladies who helped at the Mansfield YMCA. Young children can also be seen on the picture.

Ladies & soldiers at the YMCA Mansfield

The secretary of the Mansfield YMCA had reported in May 1917 how well the soldiers had used their facilities with the following figures:[37]

| YEAR | INCOME | NUMBER OF MEALS |
|---|---|---|
| 1916 | £1,625 | 78,000 |
| 1917 | £3,444 | >165,350 |
| (Average cost of teas and suppers 3ᵈ) | | |

This in turn represented many hours of voluntary work, done mostly by women. Work that was acknowledged by the YMCA with the presentation of the Order of the Red Triangle to the ladies and a few men. The Duchess of Portland presided over the first ceremony at Mansfield in 1917 and Mr C Houfton gave out the awards in 1918. At the event in 1918 it was stated that around 300 ladies were working at the YMCA Hall in Mansfield and the huts at Clipstone Camp.[38]

Unfortunately it takes an accident for the name of just one of the YMCA lady helpers to be discovered. In October 1918 Miss Lily Shelmerdine was travelling in a motor car with three other lady helpers down the main drive to No. 3 Hut at the camp when horses attached to a transport wagon got out of control. This caused a collision in which Miss Shelmordene sitting in the front with the driver was badly injured. In the three years ladies had been travelling to the camp it was the first accident to happen.[39]

Mansfield women such as Ruth Bean was known to have worked at Clipstone Camp hospital as this post card reveals. She is recalled as being Head Cook at the hospital.[40]

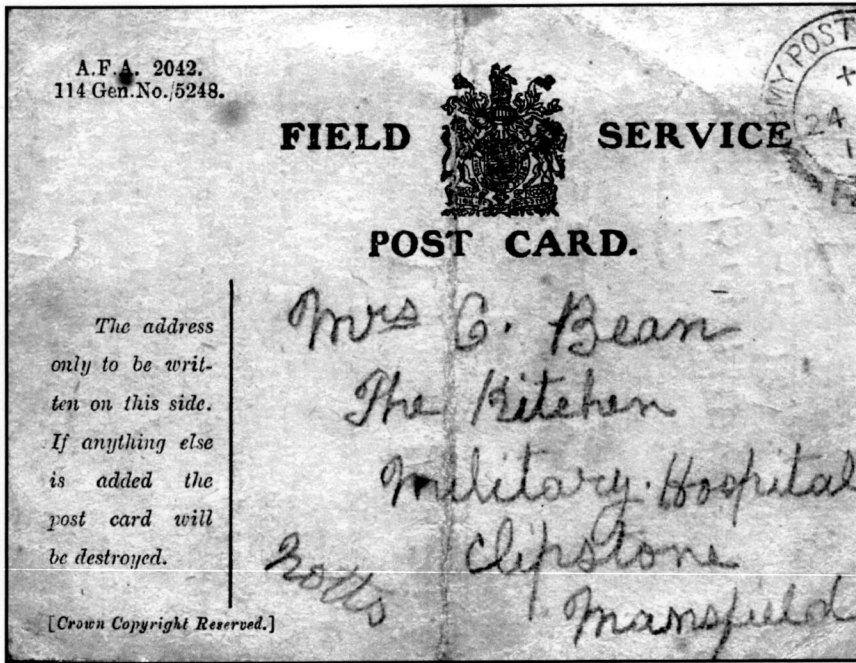

On the photograph below she is second from the right on the back row, the picture appears to be of both catering and medical staff.

Until May 1918, relatives summoned to the Clipstone Camp hospital to visit seriously ill family found accommodation for their stay was very limited. Sometimes they had to share a crowded room in the hospital, or if these were full, beds were made up for them in corridors. This and providing the visitors with meals was an additional workload for the hospital staff and an appeal for help was made to the YMCA from the officer in command.

This resulted in a hostel 'a comfortable and commodious building of wood' being provided and opened in May. The hut provided by the YMCA was at the rear of the hospital adjoining the Freemasons hut. Visitors were welcomed to the hostel by the Lady Superintendent Miss Travis who had been an active worker in the Mansfield YMCA for a long time. A local newspaper quoted 'In her new sphere she is showing the qualities of cheerfulness, sympathy, enthusiasm and good management which are essential for the position.'[41]

YMCA Hostel - Miss Emily Travis (Lady Superintendent) and Miss W M Proudlove

Towards the end of the war in June 1918 it was being suggested to local inhabitants that a club or hostel should be provided in the town for the YWCA whose emblem was a Blue Triangle. Huts were already available at Clipstone Camp to receive a large number of WAACs who were due to arrive there.[42] For the female volunteer brigades in Mansfield it was another opportunity to assist in the war.

Throughout the war, a group of influential ladies in the town were concerned in protecting young women from the influence of soldiers. With Lady Victoria Bentinck as their president they opened a Girls Club to provide young girls of a working age with somewhere to go after work. The club provided girls with opportunities to learn new skills, and to participate in recreational activities. It was also a place they could arrange to meet male friends. Local critics considered there were risks in opening such a club. The 'Ladies', however, regarded there were greater risks when men and women met casually on the streets. In recognising the 'natural desire for girls and young soldiers to meet, the club executive had endeavoured to give them an opportunity for that natural outlet.'[43] The attraction of the soldiers in uniform is remembered by an elderly Mansfield lady. She refused to walk out with local boys, preferring instead a young man in uniform who was stationed at the camp.[44] In July 1917 when the club held its first annual meeting, the success of the venture was acknowledged. Lady Victoria, Lady Markham, the Mayor and many others paid tribute to the support and hard work of the local ladies.

As in any society there were certain females who chose not to be influenced by the safe haven of a girls club. The attractions of the soldiers and the area of the camp offered more exciting prospects. An attraction that often warranted an appearance before the local magistrates.

**Mary Hunt who, 'had been living in a certain way'[45] was fined for being drunk with a crowd of soldiers in the town.**

**Lucy Green re-appeared before magistrate's for not complying with an order which prohibited her from going within a 10 mile radius of the camp.[46]**

**A similar ban was issued on Elizabeth Welton a common prostitute who was referred to as a dangerous woman. It 'was absolutely necessary she should be kept from the district'[47] as she was found in the huts at the camp, 'the soldiers having taken her there'.[48] A prison sentence of one month did not deter her. She reappeared six months later, and was sentenced to six months hard labour.[49]**

**Elizabeth Marshall, also restricted by the 10 mile ban, stated she was sorry she had returned to Mansfield when on her 67th appearance before the magistrate, she was fined 7/6d for being drunk.**

For others the attractions of soldiers led them to theft. A girl of 16 appeared before at the Petty Sessions accused of stealing her grandmother's money and spending it on the soldiers.[50] For Ellen Dean, working at the camp, temptation proved too much. She had bacon, rabbits, and army boots hidden under the piles of washing on her dray.[51]

Ellen Dean would have been just one of the women who did washing for soldiers at Clipstone Camp. This was remembered many years later by their children "mother used to do washing at Clipstone Camp for Major Draper."[52] "My mother used to collect and return officers washing in a child's pram with her friend Nellie."[53] For women such as these, the opportunity to earn extra money to help feed their families must have far outweighed the long trek to the camp and back in days when washing clothes was a major chore.

The occupations and interest of Mansfield women throughout the war developed in many different ways. Many that were advantageous to the well-being and running of the town and a few that were detrimental. Those like the military nurses, munition workers, and the women, who took over occupations of men, can be easily selected to fit into the national picture. In reality they are a minority. Nationally many women participated in volunteer work. However, for the women of Mansfield, greater opportunities arose to do this because of the military camp. They were fortunate in their local leaders. Nationally they were all part of a great team, who could be proud of their contribution to the war effort. As individual wives, mothers, sweethearts and widows, each one had their own personal war to cope with but still took the opportunity to help others. Such was the impact of war.

# END NOTES

1    Marwick A. *Women at War 1914-1918,* (1977)`p. 166.
2    ibid.                                       p. 13
3    Bourne J.M.*Britain & The Great War 1914-18,* (1989)p. 130. also        Marwick Arthur, *The Deluge: British Society and the First World War 2nd Edition,* (1971)p. 130.
4    Crute D The Industrial Development of Mansfield Since 1981, in [n.g.] *Mansfield: The Last Century,* (Nottingham 1991) p 84.
5    Marwick. *Women at War 1914-1918,* (1977) p 166.
6    Using Marwick (*The Deluge*) & Crute
7    Mansfield Reporter 4 Sep.1914, p. 8 col. 3.
8    NA  DC/M 1/1/24      (n.g.) Dec.1914
9    ibid.                        2 Dec.1915
10   ibid.                        2.Dec.1915
11   NA  DC/M1/1/26        27 Mar. 1917
12   Oral History, R. Cope daughter of Norah Brooks.
13   Mansfield Chronicle        5 Oct.1916  p. 3 col. 5
14   ibid..                     22 Mar. 1917  p. 7 col. 5
15   Mansfield Reporter        14 Jun. 1918  p. 6 col. 3
16   Mansfield Chronicle        29 Nov.1917  p. 2 col. 3
17   ibid.                      29 Jun. 1917  p. 2 col. 2
18   ibid.                       2 Aug.1917  p. 1 col. 3
19   ibid.                      10 May 1917  p. 3 col. 8
20   ibid.                       4 Oct.1917  p. 7 col. 3
21   Mansfield & District Hospital Annual Report 31 Dec. 1917 p. 6
22   ibid.                                    31 Dec. 1919 p. 8
23   Mansfield Chronicle,       22 Feb.1917  p. 1 col. 3
24   Marwick.  *Women at War 1914-1918* (1977) p 21
25   Mansfield Chronicle        22 Feb.1917  p. 1 col. 3
26   Brunts School Magazine          1918  Vol.2 No 18 pp 31-39
27   Mansfield Reporter        23 Apr. 1915  p. 5 col. 1-2
28   Mansfield Chronicle        14 Dec.1916  p. 7 col. 4
29   ibid.                      22 Jan.1917  p. 1 col. 2
30   Mansfield Reporter        18, Dec,1914
31   NA DC/MW 1/3/5/4          29 Oct.1917
32   Mansfield Chronicle        19 Jul. 1918  p. 3 col. 2
33   ibid.                       1 Jan.1915  p. 5 col. 7
34   ibid.                      13 Jul.1916  p. 2 col. 6
35   ibid..                     31 Oct.1918  p. 1 col. 5
36   ibid.                      13 Jul.1916  p. 2 col. 6
36   ibid.                      17 May 1917  p. 8 col. 6
37   ibid.                      17 May 1917
38   ibid.                      31 Oct.1918  p. 1 col. 5
39   ibid.                      31 Oct.1918
40   Oral History Mrs Winter, relative of Ruth Bean
41   Mansfield Chronicle      7 June 1918
42   Mansfield Reporter      14 June 1918  p. 6 col. 1
43   Mansfield Chronicle      20 Jul.1916  p. 3 col.,1-3
44   Oral History Mrs Brown, Forest Town Dec. 1994
45   Mansfield Chronicle      22 Feb.1917  p. 1 col. 2
46   ibid.                    20 Sep.1917  p. 8 col. 5
47   ibid.                     7 Sep.1916  p. 3 col. 5
48   ibid.                     7 Sep.1916  p. 3 col. 5
49   ibid.                    31 May 1918  p. 5 col. 1
50   ibid.                     5 July 1918  p. 2 col. 6
51   ibid.                    26 July 1918  p. 6 col. 3
52   Oral History lady at Meden Vale 10 Jan. 1994
53   Notes from Derek Johnson      2003

# 8 - WOMEN IN UNIFORM

Clipstone Camp the military training camp established near Mansfield in 1915 had for over three years been mainly occupied by thousands of soldiers in uniform. The exception being nurses at the attached military hospital. By 1918 people in the local communities were well used to seeing soldiers in their khaki uniform, flat caps and putties, they were everywhere and it could be said they were a part of local life.

CLIPSTONE ROAD, FOREST TOWN.  NO. 2.

**Soldiers walking from Clipstone Camp
through Forest Town towards Mansfield**

However from June 1918 additional uniforms would be seen when members of the Women's Army Auxiliary Corps, [WAACs] were stationed at Clipstone Camp. The WAACs were the first army unit for women and were founded in July 1917. The idea was that they could take over some of the lighter work [administration etc.] done by men so that they could be sent to play a more active part in the war.

The WAACs uniform was a khaki jacket and skirt plus a tight fitting cap. The length of the skirt had to be no more than 12 inches above the ground.[1] These women in uniform were soon to be found in camps all over England including the one at Clipstone.

The Mansfield Reporter Newspaper in June 1918 reporting on a meeting about the work of women during the war, told readers:-

*'The work of the WAACs both in France and at home, was simply first class. Not only did they attend to comforts of the soldiers, but they released men to go out and do proper men's jobs of fighting and helped in a hundred different ways. One saw them in camps in England doing all sorts of jobs that one never used to think of being women's work... There is a large camp at Clipstone...the huts are ready and in a few weeks a large number of WAACs will arrive. A certain number have already arrived and when we get hundreds more up at this bare camp they will come down to the town and stroll and see the shops. It is up to*

*you the inhabitants of Mansfield to provide a club or hotel here, so that the girls will have a place where they can have a bit of rest and recreation and where they can take their friends.'* [2]

The inference of a 'bare camp' suggests that less soldiers were there than in previous times, even though new contingents did keep arriving.

The local community was now being urged to look after the WAACs as they had done for the soldiers by providing recreational huts. They were also being made aware of the YWCA [Young Women's Christian Association] who were ready to administer to the needs of the women soldiers.

Appeals for YWCA Huts were launched which would carry the sign of the Blue Triangle as apposed to the Red Triangle for soldiers. Local collieries were soon raising money for the 'Hut Fund'. Concerts were held at the Grand Theatre, and the Old Meeting Room Schoolhouse in Mansfield. It was known the money would be wisely and well spent.[3] In November 1918 a WAACs Rest Room was opened in Mansfield by Lady Victoria Bentink. It was said that even though the hostilities had ceased, there was still many months of work ahead for the girls with demobilisation taking place and this was where they could enjoy rest and recreation.[4]

While very little is known about the WAACs and their time at the camp one former soldier stationed at Clipstone Camp recalled them in his memories. He referred to them as being 'clerks, cooks, waitresses in the officers mess and cleaners for the church, theatre etc.' [5] He also spoke of the women being in enclosed huts suggesting their accommodation was separated from that of the soldiers.

WAACs unlike soldiers, were not given officer ranks, instead they had Controllers and Administrators. Forewomen were the equivalent of NCOs and it has been suggested that these were from working class women while the more senior posts were from higher class backgrounds.

Some WAACs obviously objected to the cleaning side of the work they were given as an article in the Nottingham Evening Post 5th December 1918 revealed.

> **INSUBORDINATE WAACs**
>
> **REFUSED TO SCRUB**
>
> **THE COOK HOUSE FLOOR**

Olga Mary Brailsford and Gertrude Baxter had been given orders by Alice Stewart (Administrator of the corps), and Alice Samuel (forewoman of a cookhouse), to scrub the cookhouse floor with soap and water. The girls objected to this stating the floor was so rough and uneven and was not fit to scrub on their hands and knees, instead they swilled the floor with water and a bass (sic) broom.

It appears that sixteen girls in the cookhouse had been given the order and only two obeyed it, however because 'there had been so much insubordination amongst these girls the commanding officer was compelled to take action.' Because Olga Mary Brailsford and Gertrude Baxter were classed as ringleaders they were the ones taken before the magistrates at Mansfield Petty Sessions for 'wilfully neglecting their duties on November 2nd.' The girls were fined ten shillings and sixpence and told it was a serious offence to disobey a military order.

As women in the WAACs were not given full military status, breaches of discipline were not punished in a military court.

## SOLDIERS WIFE AND THE WAAC
### Husband Objected To Her Serving

One of the earliest occasions the Mansfield magistrates had WAACs appearing before them was in January 1918, (before contingents of WAACs had arrived at Clipstone Camp). Frances Towers was charged with absenting herself from a training centre for the WAACs which she had joined the previous October. After being given two weeks leave to see her soldier husband who was home from France she had sent her uniform back thinking she could give two weeks notice! when he objected to her enlisting. She was to appear before the Bench at a later date. [6]

Another woman who gave her name as Margaret Maclean (real name Tunnicliffe) was charged with obtaining board and lodgings at two Mansfield addresses, stated she had gone to London to join the WAACs but had left as she was not satisfied with the food. Because this lady had previous convictions she was sentenced to three months in prison.[7]

For some WAACs and soldiers their names were recorded for happier reasons as the Edwinstowe Parish Registers reveal two marriages of brides and grooms who were both stationed at the camp. Both couples were married on 12th December 1918.

| | | |
|---|---|---|
| **Grewcock** Percy | Soldier | Clipstone Camp |
| **Cockcroft** Anne Marion | WAAC | Clipstone Camp |
| | | |
| **Brooks** Walter | Soldier | Clipstone Camp |
| **Lock** Eva Winifred | WAAC | Clipstone Camp |

To date [2013] no photographs have been discovered of WAACs either at the camp, or in the Mansfield area. Additionally unlike the knowledge we have of thousand of soldiers being at Clipstone Camp, the only indication relating to the number of WAACs is that hundreds were expected.[8]

The WAACs were soon to be joined by other groups of women at Clipstone Camp. These were members of the NAACB (Navy and Army Canteen Board). An indication of the work these women may have undertaken is given by an advert in the Nottingham Evening Post 28th October 1918.

**WANTED IMMEDIATELY
FOR ARMY CANTEENS**

Female Charge Hands, Waitresses, Cooks and Kitchen Maids
good wages given references required.

Apply by letter only to
Army and Navy Canteen Board, Dunham Chambers,
Pelham Street, Nottingham
or nearest Employment Exchange.

Once again women taking over this work released soldiers for other duties. These women also wore a uniform of a jacket skirt and a brimmed hat. Gloves complimented the outfit.

This picture taken of NAACB ladies at Clipstone Camp reveals that the uniform did vary according to rank, it also suggests that as in the WAACs, rank depended upon social class.

While there is no indication of the date of this and the following photograph, they are surmised to be circa 1918/19.[9]

Inspection NAACB Clipstone Camp

Apart from photographs which show an inspection of the members of the NAACB no specific documentation has been found regarding these women at Clipstone Camp.

Documented information about the work of women in World War One, is in a minority. It is known that many women worked in the nursing profession either in Queen Alexandra's Imperial Military Nursing Service [QAIMNS], in the Red Cross or as VADs [Voluntary Aid Detachment]. They worked in hospitals overseas and at home, that were specifically designated military hospitals such as the one at Clipstone Camp which had 350 beds.

While an occasional reference to the hospital at Clipstone Camp can be found, the mention of any of the uniformed nurses that worked there is very limited or indeed male members of the RAMC (Royal Army Medical Corps). However three nurses were given special recognition for their valuable nursing service in connection with the war services there.[10] The awards were sanctioned by His Majesty King George V and notification appeared in the London Gazette on the following dates.

6th April 1919 Awarded Royal Red Cross, 1st Class
Miss Cecilia Alice Stevens, A/ Matron, QAIMNS Mil. Hosp.
Clipstone Camp Notts.

31st July 1919 Awarded Royal Red Cross, 2nd Class
Miss Amy Gore Nicholls, Acting Sister, QAIMNS
Clipstone Camp Military Hospital, Notts.

31st July 1919 Awarded Royal Red Cross, 2nd Class
Miss Nellie Tuck, QAIMNSR
Clipstone Camp Military Hospital, Notts.

<u>31st July 1919 Awarded Royal Red Cross, 2nd Class</u>
Mrs Bertha Chain Edwards, Nurse, VAD
Clipstone Camp Military Hospital, Notts.

Nurse Celia Alice Stevens became Matron at Clipstone Camp Hospital on the 25th September 1916, she was aged 38. She remained there until September 1918 when she moved to a Military Hospital at Aylesbury saying she was very sorry to leave Clipstone as she had been very happy there.[11]

Correspondence then suggests Miss M Percival is Matron at Clipstone and Nurse Amy Gore Nicholls aged 36 arrives on the 12th October 1918 as Acting Matron. She leaves around June 1919 to serve overseas.[12]

Nellie Tuck was a nursing sister at Clipstone and was there from March 1918 to June 1919. She left Clipstone to return to Newfoundland where she was born. It was decided not to replace her, possibly because the closure of the hospital and the camp were in sight.[13]

Nothing more is known about the VAD nurse Mrs Bertha Chain Edwards apart from her mention in the London Gazette in 1919.

One other nurse that worked at Clipstone was Ada Elizabeth Young who enlisted as a VAD with the Red Cross in September 1917. All her time nursing was spent at Clipstone Camp Military Hospital,[14] and this is where on the 15th July 1918 she died of pneumonia, influenza and cardiac failure. She was aged 33. Her home address was Dublin but three days later Ada Young was buried in the churchyard of St. Alban's, Forest Town. Although for the previous 10 months she had spent her time nursing and caring for sick soldiers, she wasn't given the privilege of being buried beside them, possibly because she was a VAD not a military nurse. She lies in a corner of St Alban's churchyard near the main entrance.

Memoriam
Ada Elizabeth Young, B.R.C.S.
Of
The Voluntary Aid Detachment
Died at
Clipstone Camp
Military Hospital
On
July 15TH 1918,
Aged 33 years.
This Tablet was erected
By her Colleagues of the
Army Nursing Service

At the Easter Sunday service in April 1919 a special tribute was made to Nurse Ada Young when a brass plaque was placed on the south wall inside St Alban's Church by her nursing colleagues. The Last Post was played and the plaque unveiled in the immediate presence of Brigadier General R M Ovens (General Officer commanding the troops at Clipstone), he was accompanied by Lieut-Col Longhurst (medical officer at the camp), Rev H Bull, two lieutenants and a small company of nurses from the hospital. A detachment of soldiers from the camp were among the many people present at the service.[15]

Photographs of local women in nursing uniforms or nurses at Clipstone Camp Military Hospital are very limited. Just four have been discovered so far.

Left and above show Rhoda Hamilton Pott who worked as a nurse and a cook at Clipstone Camp. The photo (bottom left) of the nurses with a Padre are from Ruth Beans photo collection. As Ruth was a cook at Clipstone Camp and never worked anywhere else, it is assumed to be at the camp.

Written on the reverse of this photograph
*Kind Remembrance from Alyse Holding*
*Clipstone Camp April 30th 1920*

Three of the ladies in the photograph below are wearing identical clothing, the other could be their supervisor, but to which group they belong is unknown. All that is written on the back of the picture is 'Christmas 1918, Clipstone Camp'.

While very little is known of women in uniform in the Mansfield area or at Clipstone Camp during the years of the Great War, it has been revealed that there were substantial groups of them. And for many, while their names, personal information and images remain hidden, these women were a valuable part of this area's history.

# END NOTES.

| | | |
|---|---|---|
| 1 | www.spartacus.schoolnet.co.uk/Wwaac.htm | |
| 2 | Mansfield Advertiser | 14 Jun. 1918 |
| 3 | ibid. | 14 Jun. 1918 |
| 4 | Mansfield Chronicle | 21 Nov. 1918 |
| 5 | Memories of Lance Corporal Frank Henry Whatling G30448 posted on the Great War Forum by his grandson 'Andy' | |
| 6 | Nottingham Evening Post | 16 Jan. 1918 |
| 7 | ibid. | 7 Aug. 1918 |
| 8 | Mansfield Advertiser | 14 Jun. 1918 |
| 9 | On 1 Jan. 1921, the Navy and Army Canteen Board formed the nucleus of the NAAFI. | |
| 10 | The London Gazette | Apr. & Jul. 1919 |
| 11 | TNA:PRO WO 399 7936 | |
| 12 | TNA:PRO WO 399 6192 | |
| 13 | TNA:PRO WO 399 8466 | |
| 14 | Information from Red Cross Archives 2004 | |
| 15 | Mansfield Advertiser | 25 Apr. 1919 |

East Surrey's at Clipstone Camp in the final years
March 1919

# 9 - THE CLOSING YEARS

In 1918 thousands of soldiers had already taken part in the 'Great War', and for many it was the end of their lives. Many more were still arriving at military training camps such as the one at Clipstone Camp near Mansfield in Nottinghamshire to be instructed in the art of combat and warfare. It is reasonable to say that none of what they learnt could have fully equipped them for some of the horrors they would encounter during the years of the war.

12th Platoon C Coy 52nd West Yorks. Rgt. Clipstone March1918

Members Sgts. Mess 51st Notts & Derby's. Clipstone Nov. 1918

People in the local communities that surrounded camps like Clipstone could be forgiven for the image they had of the war. They only saw thousands and thousands of soldiers move in and out of the area, infiltrating the countryside as they did their training, and visiting the towns and villages for recreation and social activities.

Newspapers were the main source of information for the majority of the population in those years of the First World War unlike today [2013] when modern technology brings us instant pictures of conflicts at home and abroad, and very little is left to our imagination.

The vast wooden complex of Clipstone Camp established in 1915 had expanded and improved over the years. For soldiers entering Clipstone Camp in 1918 it was said to be 'quite a comfortable camp... with good stoves in the huts, electric light, and you can get a bath...[1] This was a stark contrast to the first arrivals in 1915 when the camp had no electricity and was poorly equipped.[2]

Throughout the years of the camp and until the camp finally closed, the needs of those stationed there had to be catered for. The mention of military camps such as Clipstone were a regular feature in the classified columns of newspapers, as 'Tenders' were put out for supplies.

---

**ARMY CONTRACTS**

SEALED Tender for Washing and Repairing Bedding for a period of 4 months from June 1st, 1918, at the following Stations in the North Midland District:—

CLIPSTONE CAMP & COAL ASTON & GREENHILL,

also remaking of bedding, etc., at the following stations:—

NOTTINGHAM, LEICESTER, DERBY,
DONINGTON P.O.W. CAMP, KEGWORTH P.O.W. CAMP
CLIPSTONE CAMP, COAL ASTON AND GREENHILL,

will be received at the under-mentioned office until 12 o'clock noon on Thursday, 23rd May, 1918.

Forms of Tender and all information may be obtained on application to the Officer Commanding, Army Service Corps, North Midland District, 91 Burton-Road, Derby.

---

Derby Daily Telegraph Feb. 6th 1918

Tenders for food such as potatoes and frozen beef can also be discovered over the next two years.

When the armistice was declared on 11th November 1918 it is unknown of how the news of this was received at the camp, it can only be surmised there would have been joyous celebrations. Schools celebrated with giving children a brief holiday. St John's School, Mansfield poignantly recorded '11th November 1918 Armistice signed, children sang National Anthem, - school closed for rest of the day'. At Forest Town school children were granted a half day holiday on the 12th November in honour of the declaration of the armistice.[3] (The Mansfield Chronicle newspaper published on the 14th November did not carry large headlines declaring the end of the war. Instead it concentrated on telling readers of thanksgiving services and bazaars that were being planned to celebrate this long waited for event.

While the local communities could now look forward to celebrating the return of their surviving families who had been fighting for king and country, they were not to see an immediate demise of soldiers at Clipstone Camp. Hundreds (possibly thousands) of soldiers would continue to move in and out of the camp even though the war had officially ended. Men from 51 KOYLI (Nov 1918), 52nd Leicester's (Dec 1918), 53rd Notts & Dbys (Dec 1918), 5th Mddx (Mar 1919), Royal Fusiliers (April 1919), East Yorks (July 1919), and many more were at the camp and still in the Mansfield area.

H. Coy 2nd Lincolns, Clipstone May 1919

Thousands of soldiers knew Clipstone Camp and the area around it because that was where they had spent weeks and months training, others just knew it as a place where they were sent to be demobbed. At the end of the war the camp became one of the biggest dispersal centres in the country - known as both No 2 and No 3 Dispersal Unit Clipstone. A soldiers time at the Dispersal Unit would be short, and his surroundings would have been of very little interest. Clipstone Camp was a means to an end - handing in army equipment, obtaining necessary documents to leave the army and start a new life in 'civvy street.'

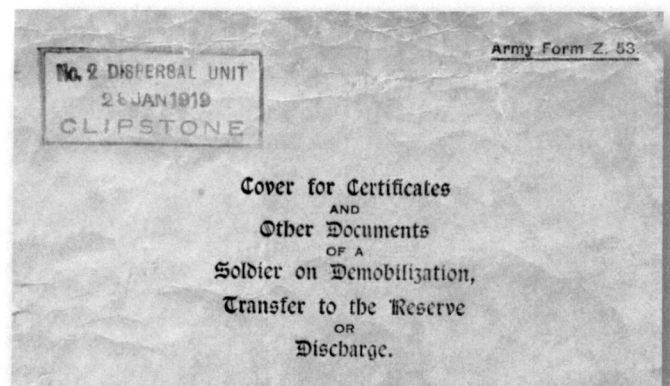

For many this journey to Clipstone Camp was a long one as the examples below reveal:-

Private David Stockdale KOYLI travelled from France in February 1919, landed at Tilbury Docks, London, then on to Clipstone and finally home to Yorkshire on 6th February.[4]

Private Hartley Hogarth No. 025831 Royal Army Medical Corps travelled from Egypt to Clipstone Camp, via Italy, Le Havre, then England.[5]

For 28 year old Private Charles Percy Finney of the Royal Warwickshire Regiment returning home after serving three years in Mesopotamia, Clipstone Camp was the end of his journey. He died there on 11th March 1919, his brothers and sisters in Woodend Tamworth, paid tribute to him in their local newspaper.[6]

The conditions some soldiers travelled home in were horrendous; travelling in a truck for seven days without comfort or convenience. Soldiers packed in horse boxes for an eight day journey with the door open to let air in, or packed seven days and nights in cattle trucks after which they pitched tents in the rain and later had a six mile march followed by a boat journey. Eventually they arrived at Clipstone Camp to be given their demobilisation papers.

Sadly for some such as Corporal Harry Atkinson No. 110411 Tank Corps, Samuel Whitaker 10th Battalion West Riding Regiment, and Private Hartley Hogarth No. 025831 Royal Army Medical Corps, the journey and the conditions endured was too much, they all died of illness within a few hours/days of reaching their homes in Yorkshire. Their deaths resulted in questions being asked in the House of Commons in March 1919.[7]

One young lad who had lived in the cottages across from Clipstone Camp since 1915, in later years [1990] recalled seeing the growth of the camp including the camp station, soldiers digging trenches, going on route marches. However at the end of the war when he was twelve years old he saw soldiers being brought to Clipstone to be demobbed. "We saw some awful sights... we used to go to the railway station to watch them get off the train, oh we did see some... and still only about eighteen years old, some of the lads were."[8]

Another ten year old boy Eric Beadsmoore who in March 1919 moved from Nottingham with his family to live in the cottages at Clipstone, was also as a young lad very much aware that even though the war was over the camp was still very active and was being used as a demobilisation centre. However, it was not the horror he remembered but the pageantry when the troop trains came in. The arrival of a Scottish Regiment was impressive, "the band formed up on the road, first about twenty fifes and I think about ten side drums, two big drums - the drummers, big men with leopard skins then twenty or so bagpipes. The soldiers forming up behind, hundreds of them all wearing kilts which I had never seen before. They marched away into the camp." [9]

There were many sights and memories relating to the soldiers and the camp that people would not forget. For some it would be a visit to the Military Hospital to see their sick or dying relative. In October 1918 many had pneumonia and an appeal in the Mansfield Chronical newspaper told readers it was a matter of life and death for the hospital to obtain new laid eggs. It was said that:-

*'Men were dying for the want of them. The resources of the hospital are being taxed to the uttermost by the large number of lads dangerously ill with pneumonia. Fresh eggs have a very important place in the battle against death, and the hospital authorities find them almost unobtainable'[10] Eggs could be sent to the Matron at the camp or left at Willman's on White Hart Street, Mansfield.*

Two weeks later an acknowledgement was placed in the paper by H H C Dent, Lieut. Col. RAMC (TF) Officer in Charge, Military Hospital, Clipstone Camp, thanking people for their donations of eggs. A list shows how people responded and who had access to fresh eggs.

| | |
|---|---|
| Mansfield Papers | Mr Houfton |
| Chaplain Wier | Mrs Cumberland, Mansfield |
| Mrs Cox, Mansfield | Miss Birks YMCA |
| Miss Dodsley, Stoney Houghton | Vicar of Edwinstowe |
| Mrs Bosworth, Sutton-in-Ashfield | Little Matlock Mills |
| Miss Marlow, Mansfield | Other anonymous donors |
| Miss Hallam, Allamore Farm, Farnsfield | |

The needs of the hospital and camp continued to be advertised in the classified columns of newspapers such as the Derby Evening Telegraph 23rd February 1920 bringing a stark awareness that soldiers were still dying fifteen months after the war had officially ended.

---

**ARMY CONTRACTS**

TENDERS are invited for the performance of Military Funerals at the under-mentioned stations in the North Midlands District, for a period of 12 months, commencing 1st April 1920.

| | |
|---|---|
| LICHFIELD | LINCOLN |
| LEICESTER | CRANWELL, Lincs. |
| DERBY | NOTTINGHAM |
| GRANTHAM | CLIPSTONE CAMP, Notts. |
| BROCTON CAMP | RUGELEY CAMP |

Forms of Tender and all information may be had on application to the Officer Commanding, Army Service Corps, North Midland District, Normanton Barracks, Derby.

Tenders will be opened at the above mentioned Office at 12 noon on Friday, 27th February 1920

---

Any death as a result of the war is regrettable and those from tragic accidents in and around the camp more so. Sadly even as late as July 1919 this still happened when Pte Reginald Alfred Bell of the East Surrey Regiment was fatally wounded in a shooting accident at the camp. He was only 18 years old. Pte C Alexander was also wounded in the accident.[11]

Pte Bell was buried in St Alban's Churchyard, Forest Town, the nearest churchyard to the camp. This is where 27 soldiers and one VAD nurse - all from Clipstone Camp lie. Locally it is said that these 27 soldiers died of influenza, however this is open to question as some are known to have died from other causes, such as accidents, TB, and bronchitis.

**War graves of soldiers from Clipstone Camp in St Alban's Churchyard Forest Town, 2012**

TR5/222468 PRIVATE
G. GILBOURNE
KING'S OWN YORKSHIRE L.I.
20TH NOVEMBER 1918 AGE 18

Soldiers who are recorded as dying at Clipstone Camp, are not just buried locally, others are buried/commemorated far and wide such as:

Bratton Baptist Chapel Yard, Wiltshire, Sighthill (Eastwood) Cemetery, Glasgow, Fullham Palace Cemetery, London., Hill Top Cemetery, Leeds., St Helen's Churchyard, Pinxton, Derbyshire, St Mark's Churchyard, Cromford and Mansfield Cemetery, these are just a few examples, there are many more.[12]

⇐ Pinxton Derbyshire

Mansfield Cemetery ⇒

REV. S. DUNSTAN
CHAPLAIN TO THE FORCES
4TH CLASS
16TH JULY 1918

- 116 -

By March 1920 it was becoming evident the camp as such was no longer needed. The Mansfield Reporter newspaper on the 26th March referred to it as:-

## 'A Deserted Camp'

Today there are only 100 ranks quartered at the Clipstone Camp. The rear parties of the 16th HLI 53rd Gordons and 19th East Surreys left the camp on Tuesday, most of the personnel being for demobilisation. Only a few RASC men and the camp headquarters detail are left. Since this time last year when the camp was one of the biggest centres in the dispersal organisation, there has been a gradual diminution in numbers quartered at Clipstone.

It is not known definitely whether any new personnel is likely to arrive at Clipstone, it is considered improbable that the camp will be occupied by any large troops.'

14 Platoon 'D' Coy. 51st Gordons February 1920
These were among some of the last soldiers at Clipstone Camp

It became evident the camp had served its purpose and adverts were placed in newspapers far and wide selling the huts.

**MINISTRY OF MUNITIONS**

By direction of the Disposal Board
(Huts and Building materials section)

**TWO DAY SALE OF ABOUT
150 HUTS AND OTHER BUILDINGS**
At No 5 and 8 Lines
**CLIPSTONE CAMP**
2 Miles from Mansfield, 12 Miles from Nottingham
and near Clipstone Station (GCR)

on MONDAY and TUESDAY
17th & 18th May
at One pm daily

Western Daily Press Bristol, Saturday May 8th 1920

The advert went on to describe the huts, what they were made of and what they had been used for:

> 72 Excellent Huts used as men's Quarters, Two Regimental Institutes, Church Hut, Six Officers Quarters, Four Officers Mess Huts, Two QMS Huts, Four Officers Kitchens, Two Baths and Boiler Houses, Two Large Cook Houses, Four Excellent Drying Rooms, Two Guard Rooms, Two Company Offices. Additionally there were horse shelters, forage sheds, coal and wood compounds, cooking ranges, 40 gallon farm boilers, iron baths etc.

This sale was just for two of the Lines, there would be others as the numbers of soldiers were depleted and the camp dismantled. Catalogues were printed and people could view the items on selected days before the sales.

Once again as in 1915, the roads around the area would have been congested with traffic and people. In 1915 the camp scenario was one of huts being built, in 1920 it was one of huts being dismantled and taken away. An extract from a Warsop man's diary gives an insight into this.[13]

*1920 DIARY of Frank Blythman  (Blythman Bros Warsop)*

| | |
|---|---|
| 19 Oct. Tuesday | Went to Clipstone Camp afternoon |
| 21 Oct. Thursday | Went to Clipstone Camp & bought a Hut No 86 for £52 paid Bradwell & Son Auctioneers. |
| 25 Oct. Monday | Started to take roof off of hut at Clipstone Jim Riley with us. |
| 26 Oct. Tuesday | Taking roof off Jim Riley with us. |
| 27 Oct. Wednesday | Finished taking roof off & gables. Bought a Rip Saw for the job. |
| 28 Oct. Thursday | Jimmy Riley did not turn up. Took one side down. |
| 29 Oct. Friday | Jim did not come. John & I took side & both ends down, only floor left. |
| 30 Oct. Saturday | John cutting floor up |
| 2 Nov. Tuesday | Cutting floor up & pulling nails out<br>Someone pinched the fittings |
| 3 Nov. Wednesday | Nail pulling & getting lorry. Bought two Stoves 25/- each. |
| 4 Nov. Thursday | Fetched the Hut from Clipstone Camp, paid Wright of Woodhouse £5 for lorry & two men one day. |
| 5 Nov. Friday | Put floor of Hut up |
| 6 Nov. Saturday | Put walls of Hut up<br>paid one man Bateman  15/- for 1½ day<br>paid another 30/- 3 days<br>    John £3 |
| 13 Nov. Saturday | Put ridge on Hut |
| 6 Dec. Monday | Putting Boards on Hut. Jacked Roof up. |
| 7 Dec. Tuesday | On Hut Boarding |
| 8 Dec. Wednesday | Putting 3 ply on Hut |
| 9 Dec. Thursday | Hut morning fixing 3 ply |
| 15 Dec. Wednesday | Went to Warsop then to Mansfield on Eastwoods lorry, bought wire for Hut windows ordered Tunnel Wire £2–0–0 |
| 18 Dec. Saturday | Paid Jimmy Riley £1–16–0 for work at Clipstone Camp |

The writer of the diary, Frank Blythman was demobbed from Clipstone Camp. The Hut was believed to have been erected on Ridgeway Road, Warsop, Notts.

Once again, (as in 1915) Clipstone Camp became a topical issue of the Mansfield Woodhouse Council in 1920. The possible purchase of huts for temporary living accommodation was considered. Additionally they were considering the purchase of a portion of the camp hospital when this was offered for sale.[14] The outcome of this is unknown.

The sinking of Clipstone Colliery which had been halted at the outbreak of war in 1914 resumed at an unknown date in 1920, (coal was eventually reached in April 1922). When the work at the colliery restarted, accommodation was needed for some of the workers and some of the army huts were utilised for this purpose. Instead of soldiers the huts now housed families of colliery workers, and some of the first children of the new Clipstone village were born in them. Children of school age such as George and William Lancaster attended the school in Forest Town, their address in October 1921 was given as The Huts Clipstone Camp.[15] An army hut was eventually adapted as a village school in Clipstone.

This was the foundation of the Clipstone Colliery Village where eventually, in keeping with the company policy, substantial houses were built for colliery workers and their families by the Bolsover Colliery Company. The early years for both the workmen and their families moving into the new village would have been a time of possible confusion, if not chaos. The area had two separate major activities taking place with the sinking of the coal mine and gradual demolition and sale of the vast wooden army camp with its hundreds of huts and related equipment. The noise, dust and dirt of these two industrial episodes is hard to imagine.

Throughout 1921 notices continued to appear as the camp was being demolished and sold off. The Nottingham Evening Post in March 4th 1921 carried the following advert for surplus fuel etc.

---

**TENDER**

Tenders are invited for the undermentioned Surplus Fuel, etc. lying at Clipstone Camp, Mansfield:

**About 107 tons FUEL WOOD**
**About 6 tons COKE**
**About 5 cwts CANDLES**

**The above may be viewed on application to the Barrack Officer, Clipstone Camp, by appointment.**

Sealed Tenders marked 'Tender for Stores, Clipstone Camp,' should be sent to reach the undermentioned Office by 12 noon on Monday, the 14th March 1921, addressed to Officer Commanding, Royal Army Service Corps, Headquarters, North Midland Area, 15 Tenant Street, Derby

---

When the closure of the Military Hospital took place catalogues gave prospective buyers itemised lists of what could be purchased. Known sales took place in April and September 1921.

G. R.

**Ministry of Munitions.**

**By Direction of the Surplus Government Property Disposal Board (Furniture Section).**

# MILITARY HOSPITAL & STORE LANE,
# CLIPSTONE CAMP,
## NEAR MANSFIELD.

### CATALOGUE OF SALE OF
#### MISCELLANEOUS
# STORES & FURNITURE,

To be Sold by Auction, by

# Messrs. J. H. Bradwell & Sons,

ON

# TUESDAY and WEDNESDAY,
# APRIL 12th & 13th, 1921.

Sale to Commence at TEN o'clock each day.

The Goods may be viewed on Monday, April 11th, between the hours of 9.0 o'clock and 4.0 o'clock.

Further Particulars may be obtained from the Controller, Furniture Section, Ministry of Munitions, Disposal Board, Block "O," Earls Court Exhibition, London, S.W.5 ; or from the Area Disposal Officer, Hotel De Ville, King Street, Leeds; or of the Auctioneers, Thurland Street, Nottingham and Mansfield.

*"Reporter" Co., Ltd., Printers, Church Street, Mansfield.*

**G.**  **R.**

By direction of the Disposal Board (Huts and Building Materials Section).

## Military Hospital,

# CLIPSTONE CAMP,

### NEAR MANSFIELD, NOTTS.

## CATALOGUE OF SALE

OF

# HOSPITAL WARDS,

**Administrative Block, Officers' Wards, Operating Theatre, Dining Rooms, Kitchens, Nurses & Matrons' Quarters, Q.-M. Stores, Double - Oven Cooking Ranges, & Portable Farm Boilers, Enamelled Iron Baths, Glazed Sinks, Lavatory Basins, Glazed Sluices, Vertical Boilers, Clothes Racks, Dressers, Cupboards, &c.,**

**TO BE SOLD BY AUCTION, BY**

# Messrs. J. H. Bradwell & Sons,

## On TUESDAY, SEPT. 6th, 1921.

SALE TO COMMENCE AT 11.30 O'CLOCK.

Auctioneers' Offices :—
Thurland Street, Nottingham, & Market Chambers, Mansfield.

"Reporter" Co., Ltd., Printers, Church Street, Mansfield.

Every item possible was sold off and the sale of this hospital can be compared to that of Harlow Wood Orthopaedic Hospital near Mansfield in 1995 when everything above and below ground was sold - the exception being the Clipstone Camp Military Hospital had a corrugated iron fencing around it which was 453yds run by 7ft. 6in. high. This was also offered for sale.

The camp huts were sold and re-used for many different purposes, village halls, schools, churches, family homes and garages. They were rebuilt locally and at a distance, one became a village hall in Scotter Lincolnshire.[16] A few can still be discovered but their original purpose has faded under new facades.[17]

For over three years since the end of the war people in the local communities had been adjusting to a life free from the fear of war. Many surviving husbands, sons, and fathers had returned home, for some it had not been an immediate return and their names appeared in the Absent Voters Lists compiled for the 1918 elections.

**Example from Mansfield /Mansfield Woodhouse Absent Voters List**

|  | Name | Address | No. | Serving |
|---|---|---|---|---|
| 1617 | MASON James | 31 Belvedere Street | 77879 | 2nd AM RAF |
| 1943 | HUTCHINSON Harry | Sherwood Hall Cottages | 29165 | Pte 7th The Buffs |
| 2549 | SMITH Henry Ilett | 36 First Avenue, Forest Town |  | ERE RN HMS 'Kent' |
| 3562 | DRING Thomas Seagrave | 29 Mill Street | 203530 | Pte 2/5th Sherwoods |
| 4333 | GOODMAN Clement | 2 Newcastle Street | 21774 | Pte 10th Notts & Derby POW |
| 4330 | HAMPSHIRE William A | Morven Ave | 825355 | Teleg., RNVR 'Bodecia 11' |
| 4424 | VAMPLEW Harry | Golf Club House Sherwood Forest | 31277 | Pte AVC |

People and businesses began to adjust, one Mansfield shop, Willman's, told its customers 'The War Is Ended' the partitions which had been in place to give soldiers privacy to write their letters and cards, had been removed, and they were now looking forward to 'Peace Trade'.[18]

Peace, thanksgiving and memorials to the fallen were now the utmost thought in peoples minds. Special services across the community were held both in churches and village halls. At Forest Town after a service in the Drill Hall a parade was then made to St Alban's Church where the 27 soldiers and one nurse were buried. A short ceremony then took place at these graves and 'each cross was connected up with ribbons of the national colours and a bunch of flowers placed on every grave, in the centre was a trophy 'Lest We Forget' as well as a magnificent wreath'.[19]

Communities did not forget but gradually the sight of men in uniforms and the large Military Camp at Clipstone became a thing of the past, the years of the Great War had finally drawn to a close.

# END NOTES.

1  Letter from Edward Rowland Litchford, 52 West Yorks. 2nd Feb. 1918 to his mother.
2  Letter from John Chesshire [sic] 27 Jun. 1915
3  Forest Town Mixed School        12 Nov 1918
4  Memories of his father David Stockdale KOYLI from Maurice Stockdale.
5  Hansard Transport Conditions *HC Deb 24 March 1919 vol 114 cc59-61W* 59W
6  The Herald [Tamworth]        29 Mar. 1919  p. 3
7  Hansard Transport Conditions *HC Deb 24 March 1919 vol 114 cc59-61W* 59W
8  Memories recorded at the Bamford Drive Oral History Group 22 Feb 1990, Facilitator Veda Kay [Librarian].
9  Memories of Eric Beadsmoore, Mansfield - visited 13 September 1994
10  Mansfield Chronicle        31 Oct. 1918
11     ibid.        17 Jul. 1919
12  This information has been found from a wide variety of sources. (See Appendix)
13  In private hands.
14  Mansfield Chronicle        20 May 1920
15  Forest Town School Admission Register
16  Information from Kenneth Green, Scotter, Linc.
17  A private garage and a bungalow in Forest Town were former huts from the camp.
18  Mansfield Chronicle        14 Nov. 1918
19     ibid.        24 Jul. 1919

# 10 - REMEMBERANCE

This book can be compared to the wearing of a poppy in November. In the words of J M Winter the wearing of a poppy, combined with the annual act of commemoration 'is to look back on an extraordinary moment in British History'.[1] The history of the First World War in Mansfield is a small but distinctive part of our national history. A history that was made significant when Clipstone Camp was established within close proximity to the town.

In Mansfield and throughout Britain, the First World War and other wars are commemorated each Armistice Day. People gather at cenotaphs and war graves, which are monuments of the past. For the military camp, that was so meaningful to the area, there is no memorial or obelisk.[2] Nationally, the camp is not well documented. Locally, it is not well-known. Both time and an expanding community have diminished the memory. However today [2013] as the centenary of the beginning of World War One approaches, a new awareness of our local military history is springing up. Information and photographs are appearing on web sites,[3] exhibitions are being planned and new publications are imminent. All will be productive in ensuring the history of the Clipstone Military camp is retained.

On the closure of the camp, the land was reclaimed for its original purpose and colliery houses eventually replaced the wooden huts. The format of the camp was retained when houses were built in avenues which followed the 'lines'[4] of the huts. The essential utility services laid to the camp could be utilised for the new village, and the service road had been improved to a reasonable standard.

In 1926 a newspaper referred to a 'village rising on the site of Clipstone Camp' when a Beer Off Licence was being applied for this new colliery village which was still in the process of being built. It now had 310 new houses, 62 bungalows, 12 colliery officials houses[5] and while other facilities were being planned it did already have a Miners Welfare Institute, a former army hut from the camp which served the community until 1933.[6]

Over the years artefacts such as broken pottery have been found in peoples gardens where once soldiers huts stood. A former local school lad recalls years ago finding a bullet on the school playing field.[7] Even today [2013] military enthusiasts are still unearthing discoveries in the area.

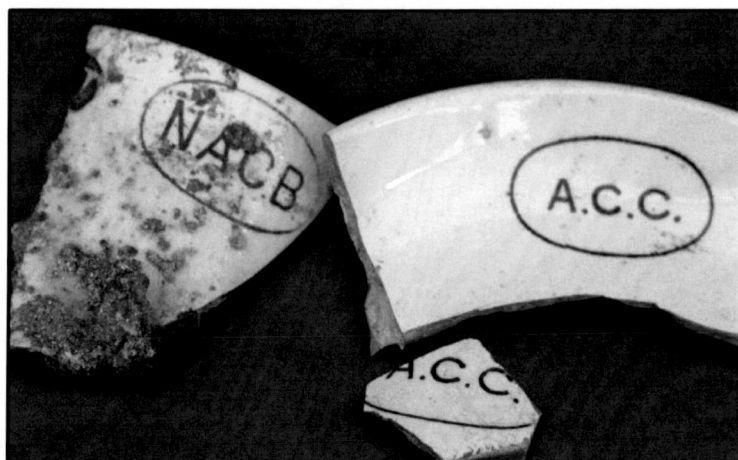

In a local forest trenches used for military training can still be discovered. Not surprisingly they have disintegrated over the years. However as the importance of these to both local and national history is realised, consideration is now being given to future renovation. The trenches were dug by soldiers over a wide area and after the demise of the camp they became play areas for young children for many years.

'There were trenches in the area, we used to play in them, some were deep, we used to play hide and seek.'[8]

That was in the 1920's and the trenches were in the area of Sherwood Golf Club.

Years later in the late 1930's trenches were still a play area for youngsters, as this memory from someone who lived on Clipstone Road, in Forest Town reveals.

'I too remember playing hide and seek in the trenches which I think had many right angles making hiding easier.'[9]

John Vamplew

When this research began over thirteen years ago, it was with the older generations that the memories remained. They were children in the years of the Great War. It was not the death and horror of the war they recalled, that war was in another land. The memories they had were of the war related to Mansfield, mostly the camp and its soldiers. An elderly man remembered soldiers billeted on the family farm.[10] His wife recalled how as a little girl, she sat on a fence near the golf course where she lived, and watched the soldiers as they marched and whistled on their way to and from the camp.

She associated them with her father John Vamplew who was in France serving in the Veterinary Corps.[11] Others recalled a teenage romance with a soldier from the camp,[12] and a brother who delivered papers there on his bike.[13] Memories of soldier's funerals and the sound of the last post had not been forgotten.[14] The war graves in the churchyard next to the school at Forest Town remain as confirmation of those ceremonies. If it had not been for Clipstone Camp, the concept of the war for the local children would have been very different.

The First World War graves of 27 soldiers from Clipstone Camp are in neat rows in St Alban's churchyard at Forest Town. They are well looked after by the Commonwealth War Grave Commission and each headstone bears the name, regiment and date of the death of the soldier. To the casual observer these are just war graves as there is nothing to indicate their connection to the military training camp that was one of the largest in the country. Separate from the rows of soldiers from the camp are the war graves of Ada Young (a Red Cross Nurse at Clipstone Camp), and Pte Harry Wilson from Forest Town who died in Lincolnshire.

In other churchyards/cemeteries such as Mansfield war graves are to be found randomly among other headstones of all shapes and sizes, unlike those at Forest Town there was nothing to warrant them being placed together.

Mansfield Nottingham Road Cemetery

In 1932 an attempt was made by Reverend Sprittles of St Alban's Church, Forest Town to have a memorial to the Soldiers of Clipstone Camp. An addition to the church was being planned, this was the north aisle and it was hoped that this could commemorate the camp in some way. Appeals to old soldiers who may have been at Clipstone, were placed in newspapers far and wide for help with funding this project. Sadly there was little response as reported in the St Alban's Page of Mansfield Woodhouse Parish Magazine, September 1932.

> *The vicar and church warden at first felt all had been in vain. 'Then two cheery letters were received from very distant and different parts of the Empire, enclosing cheques for two guineas and one pound respectively towards the building fund. The first came from Hong Kong via Siberia and the other from Bauchi Province, Nigeria, West Africa. Both of them were the result of the appeal in 'The Times'. The first came from Major-General J W Sandilands who is in command of British Troops in China. He said "I believe that I must have been the last man to command the Clipstone Camp, as I was there until March 1920... The second letter was from Erik K Featherstone, Esq who is the British Administrative Officer at Gombi in the Bauchi Province'.*

Reverend Sprittles commented that it was amazing the only two replies received came from such extremes of the Empire and felt the appeal had not been a complete failure. Eventually the North Aisle was built, and consecrated in September 1937. However it bears no reference to Clipstone Camp.

Newspapers carried memorials to those who had died in WW1 both at the time of death and for many years later. In some cases both the person and where they died are not forgotten as the example found in 'The Daily Mail [Hull] 4th November 1930' shows:-

> BRAY - In loving memory of our dear son Francis Arthur, who died Nov. 3rd 1918 at Clipstone Camp. - Always remembered.

The mention of Clipstone Camp can sometimes be remembered for unusual reasons. When a newspaper in 1948 asked its readers their thoughts about Friday 13th, Mr H F Megson replied saying he was uncertain as he recalled in the First World War;

> *'He joined the army on April 13th, was posted to Clipstone on the same day - the 13th. Was sent into the camp on the 13th line in the 13th Battalion and in the battalion he was sent to the 13th platoon. He also got 13 days CB [confined to barracks] while in the camp. He spent 13 weeks with the 13th Battalion and was sent to the 13th Machine Gun Corps. Trained there for 13 weeks before being sent to France.[15] The year wasn't given.*

An unusual memorial to Clipstone Camp, if it can be called that, is a street name in Bradford, which people living in Bradford today may not realise the origin of. This at one time would have been very meaningful to local people.

## CLIPSTONE STREET

It is understood that this street was originally named Bismarck Street which was after Otto Von Bismarck, (nicknamed the Iron Chancellor) who was the architect of German unification. Understandingly in 1916 this street name was not popular with Bradford's local residents and other suggestions were made. The residents decided they would prefer the street to be named after the West Riding Regiment in which local men had served. As a compromise the name Clipstone Street was decided on as Clipstone Camp was where many Bradford soldiers had done their training.[16] Contact was kept with those soldiers by the Lord Mayor of Bradford, to ensure the community had not forgotten them.

Clipstone Camp had a physiological affect on the people in the communities around Mansfield. It offered an opportunity to get involved in the welfare of others, and by providing many types of services for the soldiers, people had less time to be concerned with their own losses and fears. Local people turned into active citizens and became involved in the war. Alternatively, for the soldiers, the preoccupation with other people was an effective form of counselling. They had left wives and families behind and the future was unknown.

Messages in letters, on postcards, in autograph books reveal the human side of the man in uniform.

Letter from a husband

No. 6 Hut .......1. COMPANY.
13. BATTALION ROYAL FUSILIERS,
CLIPSTONE CAMP.
NOTTS.
June 29th 1915.

my darling Heart:

It was nice to get your beautiful letter this morning. the first I have had here.

This is the place all the letters are written and is very comfortable. Be good till daddy comes home again. Dad

For Correspondence

"When the leaves of this book are faded
And the writing therein is dim
Still think of me kindly
For wherever I may be
I shall alway remember You."

Billy 14.7.19

Post card from a father

Page in an Autograph Book
of YMCA Volunteer

The social and recreational activities the community provided for the soldier were an effective form of therapy. Even writing in a 'helpers' autograph book provided a way to express feelings.[17]

The loss to the community as hundreds of men enlisted and left Mansfield, was lessened by the thousands of soldiers that moved into the Clipstone Camp. They integrated into the local communities and their presence was everywhere. For the business population of the area, the soldiers' spending power was welcome. No written accounts have been discovered but very few commercial facilities would not have benefited from the custom, of either the camp, or the soldiers. The Mansfield Brewery was quick to advise major shareholders, 'the Brewery was doing well despite the war'. Into the Mansfield area had come an Army Camp of 'sixty thousand men at Clipstone'.[18] Essential supplies were necessary for the camp and these were supplied locally. Many small businesses additionally benefited from the extra money proffered by the enlarged community, they were well patronised. The YMCA, Wesleyan Methodists, and other Christian establishments were equally well supported. However, they were not aimed at profitable gain. The camp was good for the local economy.

Without the camp, businesses like the brewery may have found it difficult to survive. It was an industry already affected by restricted opening hours and a lack of custom. A large proportion of the drinking community, the miners, had enlisted in the war and the regular custom had gone with them. For the dependants of the local recruits, some employers did offer monitory support, however, this did not necessarily compare to the previous family income and could limit their spending in local shops. Some of these shops were already at a disadvantage because of restricted supplies.

MIDLAND STATION, MANSFIELD

**Posted in October 1916 this card shows the station used by soldiers in the early years of the camp. Soldiers and wagons can be seen on the left of the picture**

The existing train services from Mansfield were well patronised by soldiers from the camp, and additional trains were added for their use.[19]

A new Mansfield Railway construction was delayed due to the war, which resulted in increased expenditure and a delay in remuneration. Once this was completed it was still restricted by the number of trains it could run.

The eventual opening of a passenger service to the Clipstone Camp in October 1917 did offer some compensation. It was well patronised by the soldiers and an additional train was allowed between Nottingham, Mansfield, and the camp in January 1918.[20]

In January 1920, the phasing out of the camp was given as a contributory factor of falling profits.[21]

The opening of the Mansfield Railway's passenger service to the military camp was blamed for a decline in the local taxi service. The taxi service, however, would not have been a viable business venture if the camp had not been established near Mansfield. Similarly, applications for taxi licences would not have added to the work of the local councils.

If it had not been for the camp development the additional workload of the local councils would have been minimal throughout the war. Their expenditure would have been less and there would have been no immediate necessity to widen streets in the town. Also the health and welfare of the community would not have been at risk. A club for young girls was only initiated because of anxiety for the moral welfare of the female population, an anxiety that was produced by the excessive number of soldiers in the area. However the women of ill repute in the town would no doubt have offered their trade elsewhere.

The camp did not have any direct influence on all of the local industries. Essential war requirements kept the foundries, tin box industries, and the Shoe Company supplied with government orders; while a loss of manpower due to recruitment was blamed for a reduction in coal output. The military wards at the Mansfield Hospital were designated as part of national emergency measures for the wounded, and the wounded soldiers that came to the hospital were sent from unknown places. The local Red Cross and Voluntary Aid Detachments would still have undertaken arrangements for their care and convalescence.

The more affluent members of society, such as Lady Victoria Bentinck, rallied to the cause of the war not just the camp, and they would still have encouraged local women to work and collect for the war depots. The schools, too, would still have participated in the war effort. Some of their contributions were for the soldiers at the camp, but most of the school collections and parcels were sent to distant servicemen.

> *'Collected 55 packets of chocolate, cigarettes, OXO cubes etc. Girls made sufficient number of woollen cuffs, socks, helmets, mittens, to be included in parcels to be sent out.'[22]*

Belgium refugees arriving in Mansfield were also part of the national effort to help those who had suffered at the hands of the enemy. Local people welcomed the opportunity to help them and others. The patriotic fair in 1917 with so many participants is evidence of this.

Mansfield and surrounding villages were proud of their people who enlisted in the war. Today [2013] names on rolls of honour and cenotaphs erected after the end of the war still proclaim this. An interest in family history and local history research is ensuring information which has laid dormant in letters, diaries etc is now being made available for all to see via the internet and publications. These are all a tribute to the soldiers and their war.

Without the camp, Mansfield would still have had its war. It would have rejoiced in its VC, and held its Patriotic Fair. The civilian public would have re-acted and survived like the people of other towns in Britain, and war would have occurred at a distance.

The decision by the War Office to establish a military camp at Clipstone and move thousands of soldiers into the area effectively brought the war to Mansfield. The Camp and its soldiers changed the life of the local community. It widened the social opportunities for local people. Local business thrived, and despite the reported horrors of war, life could be exciting and prosperous; Clipstone Camp did, indeed, have a significant influence on Mansfield, in the Great War.

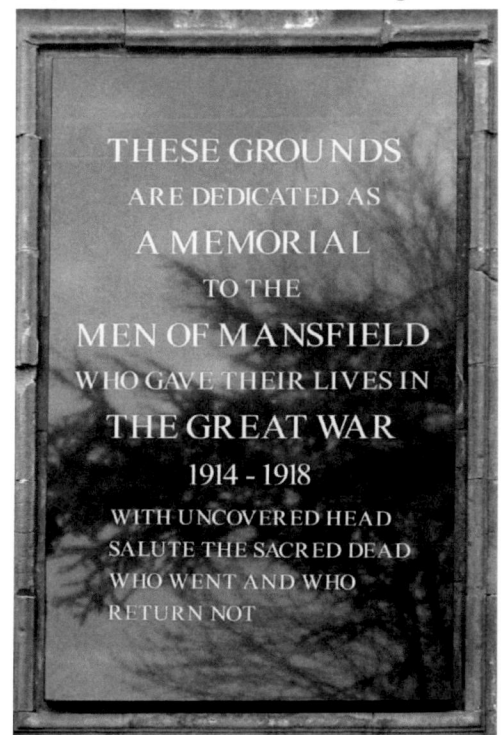

THESE GROUNDS
ARE DEDICATED AS
A MEMORIAL
TO THE
MEN OF MANSFIELD
WHO GAVE THEIR LIVES IN
THE GREAT WAR
1914 - 1918
WITH UNCOVERED HEAD
SALUTE THE SACRED DEAD
WHO WENT AND WHO
RETURN NOT

Memorial in Carr Bank Park,
Mansfield

# END NOTES.

1    J Winter, *The Great War and the British People* (1985) p 305
2    Today 2013, this is being considered by various individuals and groups in the locality.
3    See www.ourmansfieldandarea.org.uk & www.clipstonecamp.co.uk
4    The huts built in lines were used by soldiers as an address, i.e. Hut 13. 19 Lines as written on post cards. Streets at Clipstone are First Avenue, Second Avenue etc.
5    Nottingham Evening Post 11 Mar. 1926
6    ibid.                    4 Dec. 1933
7    Oral history G Marples.
8    Oral History Mrs Phyllis Newton nee Vamplew.
9    Memories R Wilkinson
10   Oral History  John Newton.
11   ibid.        Mrs P Newton.
12   ibid.          Mrs Brown.
13   ibid.          Mrs Storey.
14   ibid.          John Newton.  &  Mrs Storey.
15   The Leader Post            14 Feb. 1948
16   www.thisisbradford.co.uk
17   From Lily Chadwick's Autograph Book (in private hands).
18   As quoted in, P Bristow *The Mansfield Brew*, (Hants. 1976) p 74.
19   Mansfield Chronicle          8 Jul. 1915  p. 2 col. 4
20   TNA:PRO Rail 468/11        21 Dec.1917
21   TNA:PRO Rail 468/11        29 Jan.1920
22   Brunts School Magazine      7 Feb. 1916

# APPENDIX

## DEATHS / INQUESTS - CLIPSTONE CAMP/HOSPITAL
*These are just some of the deaths related to Clipstone Camp
that have been discovered to date (2013)*

Abbreviations used:

| | | | |
|---|---|---|---|
| Bur | = Buried | LAN | = Lancashire |
| CC | = Clipstone Camp | LDN | = London |
| Com | = Commemorated | MDX | = Middlesex |
| CWGC | = Commonwealth War Graves | NTT | = Nottinghamshire |
| | Commission | SXX | = Sussex |
| DBY | = Derbyshire | WIL | = Wiltshire |
| KEN | = Kent | YKS | = Yorkshire, |

**BAILEY** Pte. George Alfred 5362 6th Batt. Duke of Wellington's (WR Reg.). Died 10th Nov 1916 age 38. Found drowned in Flood Dykes between Old Mill Lane & New Mill Lane, [Mansfield Woodhouse]. Son of James & Ann Bailey, of Skipton YKS.

*Source CWGC/Mansfield Chronicle 16 Nov 1916/
Bur/Com. - Grave Ref 113 Morecambe & Heysham (Morecambe) Cemetery.*

**BELL** Pte. Reginald Alfred 12437 3rd Batt. East Surrey Regiment. Accidentally killed 16th July 1919 age 18. Son of Major Otto J. Bell, of 7 Palliser Court, Baron's Court, London, and the late Sybil Ormond Bell.

*Source - CWGC/Bur. St. Alban's Churchyard Forest Town. NTT.*

**BLAKEY** Pte. Walter 4785 7th Batt. Duke of Wellington's (West Riding Regt.). Died 31st May 1916 age 28. Son of George and Eliza Blakey. Born at Great Driffield, YKS.

*Source - CWGC/ Bur. St. Alban's Churchyard Forest Town. NTT.*

**BRADLEY** Lt. QM. Harry Thomas MGC (Infantry). Died 2nd April 1917 age 53. Husband of Elizabeth Bradley 16 Stanwick Road, West Kensington, London. Believed to have shot himself, found on miniature rifle range on camp.

*Source CWGC/Mansfield Chronicle 5th April 1917/
Bur. Grave ref C 11830 Nottingham Road Cemetery, Mansfield, NTT.*

**BRAY** Pte. Francis Arthur TR/5/223133 53rd Batt KOYLI. Died 3th November 1918 age 18 at Clipstone Camp. Son of Fred & Alice Bray 9 Gooderick Terrace, Cave St., Beverley Road, Hull.

*Source CWGC/Hull Daily Mail 4th Nov. (memoriam column) 1930/
Bur/Com. Grave Ref 43.21 Hull Northern Cemetery, YKS.*

**BRENT** George A/1997 AOC attd "E" Training Batt. (Clipstone) NGC. Wounded in action (France). Died 3rd September 1918 age 30 at Clipstone Camp.

*Source CWGC/www.uk-geneology/Bur/Com. Bratton Baptist Chapelyard, WIL.*

**BREW** Pte. George Edward 15864 2nd Batt. Machine Gun Corps (Inf). Died 5th December 1916 age 36. Knocked down & fatally injured by motor car on Clipstone Road, [Forest Town]. He was from Wolverhampton.

*Source - CWGC/Mansfield Chronicle 7th Dec. 1916/
Bur. St. Alban's Churchyard, Forest Town. NTT.*

**CAMERON** Pte. Ralph 203245 Royal Scotts Fusiliers. Died 15th September 1917 age 39. Train accident Clipstone Camp, son of John Cameron & Elizabeth Paul Cameron, husband of Catherine Graham Scobie Cameron 402 Baltic St. Bridgeton, Glasgow. Born Edinburgh.

*Source CWGC/Mansfield Chronicle 20th Sept. 1917/
Bur/Com. Sightill (Eastwood) Cemetery Glasgow & possibly commemorated Edinburgh.*

**CLARK** Sjt. Albert P/1882 Military Police Corps fatally injured by falling from step of a car, 15th January 1916 age 43. Inquest at CC. Son of Mr & Mrs Clark of Clewer, Windsor, husband of A L Clark of 35 Maxwell Road, Fulham. Served with Kings Dragoon Guards in South Africa Campaign.
> *Source CWGC/Mansfield Local Diary of War-Linneys Almanac/Mansfield & North Notts. Advertiser 21st January 1916/Bur/Com. Grave ref 3 G 49 Fulham Palace Road Cemetery, LDN.*

**CLARK** Pte. Frank Percy Louis T2/O/6906 3rd Reserve HT Depot (Bradford). Army Service Corps. Died of pneumonia 3rd March 1916 age 25. Son of Frederick Clark; husband of Margaret Maria Clark, of 74 Gladesmore Road., South Tottenham, LDN.
> *Source - CWGC/Bur. St. Alban's Churchyard, Forest Town. NTT.*

**COLEMAN** Pte. William 24663 Norfolk Regiment transf. to (453181) Labour Corps. Died 12th July 1918 age 31. Son of Mrs. Martha J Clarke (formerly Coleman) of 20 Orange Grove, Wisbech. Born at Harwich. Died of influenza & pneumonia.
> *Source - CWGC/Death Certificate/Bur. St. Alban's Churchyard, Forest Town. NTT.*

**COX** Frank 3130 Royal Berks. Died 10th November 1918 age 26. Son of James Stewart Cox & Annie Cox; husband of Matilda Stewart Cox, of Upper Froyle, Alton, Hants. Born at Bradfield.
> *Source CWGC/Bur/Com. Bradfield (St. Andrew) Churchyard /www.westberkshirewarmemorials.org.uk*

**CURRY** Pte. John Henry TRS/173414 53rd Batt. Durham Light Infantry. Died 9th November 1918 age 18. Native of South Shields.
> *Source - CWGC/www.military images.net/Bur. St. Alban's Churchyard, Forest Town. NTT.*

**DAVIS** Sapper William No 2 Tunnelling Depot, Royal Engineers Extension, Division 78. Died 19th May 1916 age 25. Found in the River Maun - drowned.
> *Source CWGC /Mans Chronicle 25th May 1916/ Bur/Com. Reading Cemetery, Berkshire Grave ref. 78 16223.*

**DUNSTAN** Rev Sidney Chaplain 4th Class, Army Chaplain's Department. Died 16th July 1918 age 34 - illness in CC Hospital
> *Source Web/CWGC/ Bur. Cemetery Grave Ref A 3414 Nottingham Road, Mansfield NTT.*

**ERNEST** Cpl. Alfred, 4133 6th Batt. Duke of Wellington's (West Riding Regt.). Died 30th September 1916 age 46. Husband of Ellen Smith Ernest, of 8 Dundas St., King Cross, Halifax, YKS. Born at York.
> *Source - CWGC/Bur. St. Alban's Churchyard, Forest Town. NTT.*

**ETIM** Pte. Albert, 160263. 3rd Batt. Machine Gun Corps (Inf). Died 3rd July 1918 age 21. Formerly Pte., 55349 West Yorkshire Regiment. native of Old Calabar, West Africa.
> *Source - CWGC:/www.military images.net/Bur St. Alban's Churchyard, Forest Town. NTT.*

**FINNEY** Pte. Charles Percy 15604 9th RW. Died 11th March 1919 age 28 at Clipstone Camp on his way home after serving in Mesopotamia for over three years. Native of Wood End, Tamworth.
> *Source CWGC/Bur/Com. Hurley Church Cemetery, Kingsbury/ Obituary Tamworth Herald 29th March 1919.*

**GARSIDE** Louis Robert 2715 21st Batt. Royal Fusiliers. Died 29th June 1915 age 25 taken ill at CC moved to Bagthorpe Isolation Hospital Nottingham, died of meningitis. Son of Robert and Louisa Garside, of 'Four Winds' Westfield, Battle, SSX. Born at West Wickham, KEN.

**GILBOURNE** Pte. Gerald TR/222468 KOYLI. Died pneumonia 20th Nov 1918 age 18. Son of William Gilbourne of 23 Park Lane Pinxton, DBY
> *Source CWGC/http://home.clara.net/daibevan/Bur. St. Helen's Churchyard Pinxton DBY*

**GILLOTT** Pte. William Henry 4/3402 1/4 Y & L. Died 11th April 1916 age 37 at Clipstone Camp of gunshot wound. Husband of Helen Raynes formerly Gillott 26 Crown Alley Park Sheffield. YKS
> *Source CWCG/Mansfield Chronicle April 1916/ Bur/Com. Sheffield (City Road) Cemetery, YKS.*

**GOULDSTONE** Pte. Edward 6/51608 52nd Batt. Sherwood Foresters (Notts. and Derby Regt.). Died 18th November 1918 age 18 of pneumonia.
*Source - CWGC/ Bur. St. Alban's Churchyard, Forest Town. NTT.*

**GREEN** J Pte. 203417 Royal Scots Fusiliers 4th Batt. Died train accident at Clipstone Camp 15th September 1917 age 34. Son of Peter Green of Glen Street, Paisley, husband of Maggie Dykes Green.
*Source CWGC/Mansfield Chronicle 20th Sept 1917/*
*Bur/Com. Newmilns (or Loudoun) Cemetery, Ayrshire.*

**HALSTEAD** James Driver T/293646 RASC 555th HT Coy. Died in road accident 6th February 1919 age 27. Home address 50 Mosely Street, Barnoldswick, LAN.
*Source CWGC/www.clipstonecamp.co.uk*
*Bur/Com Ghyll Undenominational Burial Ground Barnoldswick, LAN.*

**HOWELL** Pte. William Herbert G/99217. 5th Batt. Middlesex Regiment. Died 4th May 1919 age 19. Son of Mr. and Mrs. F. Howell, of Earsham, Norfolk.
*Source - CWGC/Bur. St. Alban's Churchyard Forest Town. NTT.*

**HUDSON** Pte. Percy 5929 6th Bn. Duke of Wellington's (West Riding Regt.). Died 8th November 1916 age 33. Native of Leeds, YKS.
*Source - CWGC/St Alban's Church Burial Register/*
*Bur. St. Alban's Churchyard, Forest Town. NTT./www.find a grave.com*

**HUTCHINSON** Pte. George 5673 2nd/4th Batt. Y & L. Died 13th October 1916 age 35 from heart failure at Clipstone Camp - native of Sheffield, YKS.
*Source CWGC/Mansfield Chronicle 19th October 1916/*
*Bur./Com.Wadsley Churchyard (north side of Church).*

**JACKSON** Pte. John Theodore 6375 Duke of Wellingtons. Died 13th October 1916 age unknown. Drowning/Suicide at CC. Son of WT & Mary E Jackson, of 'Morriscot' Northowram, Halifax, YKS.
*Source CWGC/Web Hansard/Bur./Com. Coley St. John Churchyard Extension.*

**LAMB** Sec. Lt. Thomas 4th (Res) KOYLI. Died 30th June 1916 age 20. He sacrificed his life to save others by seizing a live grenade dropped in trench. Inquest at CC.
*Source CWGC/ Local Diary of the War Mansfield & North Notts. Advertiser/*
*www.lorettoniansociety.org.uk/Bur/Com. Warkworth (St Lawrence) Church Burial Ground,*
*South West Old Portion 838.*

**LAWSON** Pte. Maurice Gibson TRS/173331 "A" Coy. 53rd Batt. Durham Light Infantry. Died of influenza 7th November 1916 age 18. Son of Peter Gibson Lawson and Alice Maud Lawson, of 25 Station Road, Newtown, Waltham Cross, Herts. Born at South Shields.
*Source - CWGC/Bur. St. Alban's Churchyard, Forest Town. NTT.*

**LINTON** Sjt. John, 83868. No. 4 Depot. Royal Garrison Artillery. Died 24th January 1917. age 46. Husband of Jane Linton, of 30 Churchill Road, Newtown, Great Yarmouth.
*Source - CWGC/Bur. St. Alban's Churchyard, Forest Town. NTT.*

**MALCOLM** Pte. David James, 35593. Royal Fusiliers transf. to (322553) Labour Corps. Died 17th July 1918 age 42. Husband of Jane Malcolm, of 13 Bramerton St., King's Road, Chelsea, London.
*Source - CWGC/ Bur. St. Alban's Churchyard, Forest Town. NTT.*

**MILNES** Pte. Frank 203083 Duke of Wellingtons W R Regiment 4th Batt. Died 13th April 1917 age 26 after a week's illness. Son of John & Sarah Jane Milnes. Husband of Beatrice Milnes, of 8 Kiln Lane, Slaithwaite. Born at Slaithwaite.
*Source CWGC/ Bur/Com. Grave A 4 3 Colne Valley (Slaithwaite) Cemetery, YKS.*

**MILLER** Pte. Lionel Dempster 19th Batt Royal Fusiliers. Died 12th June 1915 age 22 accident at Roscoe's Dance Hall in Mansfield NTT.

*Source CWGC/Derby Daily Telegraph Mon 14th June 1915/*
*Bur/Com. Winchester (West Hill Old) Cemetery/ United Kingdom Book of Remembrance.*

**MOORE** Pte. George Edward 61398 18th Batt. Yorkshire Regiment. Died 17th December 1918 age 22. Son of Mrs Sarah Moore, of 9 Priory Square, Mansfield Woodhouse, NTT.

*Source CWGC/Bur/Com. St. Edmund's Churchyard Extension, Mansfield Woodhouse, NTT.*

**MUIRHEAD** D Pte. 205148 Royal Scots Fusilier 4th Reserve Batt. Died 17th September 1917 age 29 - train accident at Clipstone Camp. Son of James Muirhead and Jane Walker, his widow was Susan Ireland, she had 6 children and lived at Lochfoot. He was born at Auchenfad, Auchencaien.

*Source CWGC/Scottish War Graves/Mansfield Chronicle 20th Sept 1917/*
*Bur/Com. Luchrutton Parish Churchyard, Scotland.*

**MUSGROVE** LCpl William 158644 3rd Batt. Machine Gun Corps (Inf). Died 5th July 1918 of influenza.

*Source - CWGC/ Family/ www wartimememoriesproject.com/*
*Bur. St. Alban's Churchyard, Forest Town. NTT.*

**O'LONE** Pte. James, S/19792. 1st/4th Batt. Gordon Highlanders. Died 13th August 1919 age 19. Drowned bathing at CC. Son of the late Mr. and Mrs. O'Lone. Born at Glasgow.

*Source - CWGC/Western Daily Press Bristol July 8th 1919/*
*Bur. St. Alban's Churchyard, Forest Town. NTT.*

**ORRIDGE** Sjt. Francis Arthur 168581 Railway Troops Depot (Longmoor). Royal Engineers. Died 27th August 1917 age 47. Son of Arthur and Lavina Orridge, of North Kensington, LDN.

*Source - CWGC/Bur. St. Alban's Churchyard, Forest Town. NTT.*

**PARKER** Pte. Percy Reginald 278123 2nd/6th Batt. Essex Regiment transf. to (455816) 484th Agricultural Coy. Labour Corps. Died 18th November 1918 age 20.

*Source - CWGC/St. Alban's Burial Register/Bur. St. Alban's Churchyard, Forest Town. NTT.*

**PETERS** Pte. Thomas, 55415 East Yorkshire Regiment. Died 22nd February 1918 or 1919 age 23.

*Source - CWGC/ St. Alban's Burial Register/Bur. St Alban's Churchyard, Forest Town. NTT.*

**PIDCOCK** Pte. John Arthur Sherwood Foresters. Died 27th Nov 1918 age 18 at Clipstone Camp. Son of the late Isiah [sic] and Martha Pidcock of Cromford.

*Source - CWCG/ www cromfordvillage.co.uk/ Bur. St. Marks Churchyard, Cromford DBY.*

**PIKE** Pte. George Richard 159292 3rd Batt. Machine Gun Corps (Inf). Died 7th July 1918 age 32. Son of Mrs. A. Pike, of 60 Emerald Avenue, East Ham, London.

*Source - CWGC/ St. Alban's Burial Register/Bur. St. Alban's Churchyard, Forest Town. NTT.*

**PIPER** LCpl. H 241459 Royal Scots Fusiliers 4th Batt. Died 15th September 1917 age 32. Train accident at Clipstone Camp. Husband of Sarah McConnachie , of 3 Alderston Avenue, Ayr.

*Source CWGC/Mansfield Chronicle 20th Sept 1917/Bur/Com. Ayr Cemetery, Ayrshire, Scotland.*

**PRESTON** Pte. Sam T4/235758. 212th H.T. Coy. (Clipstone Camp) Army Service Corps. Died 25th June 1918 age 28. Son of John and Mary Preston, of Rings Farm, Trawden, Colne, LAN. Husband of Annie Preston.

*Source - CWGC/ Bur. St. Alban's Churchyard, Forest Town. NTT.*

**PULLAN** Pte. Joseph 3rd/7th Battallion West Yorkshire Reg. (Leeds Rifles). Died 7th Sept.1915 age 18 drowned bathing at Clipstone Camp

*Source - CWGC/ Leeds Mercury 1915/Bur.Com Hill Top Cemetery Armley, Leeds. YKS*

**RICHARDSON** Cpl. John Henry 22nd Royal Fusiliers knocked down and fatally injured by a motor car on Clipstone Road 2nd July 1915 age 37. Husband of K L Richardson 150 Duncane Road, Acton, LDN.

*Source - CWGC/Local Diary of War & Mansfield & North Notts Advertiser 8th July 1915/*
*Bur. Nottingham Road Cemetery, Mansfield, NTT.*

**ROBERTS** Pte. Harvey 6269 3rd/6th Batt. Duke of Wellingtons Regt. Drowned 30 September 1916 age 24 believed to have committed suicide. Home address 6 Balmforth Yard, Milnes Bridge Huddersfield, YKS.

*Source CWGC/ Mansfield Chronicle 5th October 1916/*
*Bur/Com. Longwood (St Mark) Churchyard Extension, Huddersfield, YKS.*

**ROSEWELL** Pte. Henry 8057 No 8 Coy. (York), Royal Army Medical Corps. Died 3rd December 1916 age 46. Died of TB. Husband of Alice Rosewell, of 8 Bell Cottages, Charlton Road, Shepperton, MDX.

*Source - CWGC/Bur. St. Alban's Churchyard, Forest Town, NTT.*

**SIMPSON** Rifleman JOHN 8217 7th Reserve Batt. West Yorkshire Regt. (Prince of Wales's Own). Died of bronchitis 21st January 1917 age 37. Son of the late Thomas and Lavinia Simpson.

*Source - CWGC/Bur. St. Alban's Churchyard, Forest Town, NTT.*

**STOREY** Sap. Thomas William 20412 Railway Troop Depot, Royal Engineers, of 15 Russell Street, Skipton. Son of the late Mr Robert & Mary Ann Storey of 8 Chancery Lane Skipton. Died 4th January 1917 age 35 of double pneumonia and pleurisy. Husband of Sarah Ann Storey of 13 King Street, Skipton, she was with him at Clipstone Camp Hospital when he died.

*Source - CWGC/ Craven web site (Craven Herald)/*
*Bur/Com. Skipton (Waltonwrays) Cemetery, YKS.*

**STORK** Pte. Willie TR5/124064 Training Reserve 84th Batt. Died Clipstone Camp 23rd July 1918 age 20. Son of Mr & Mrs Matthew Stork of Low Ackworth.

*Source - CWGC/Pontefract & Castleford Gazette via John Ferguson/*
*Bur/Com. Ackworth (St. Cuthbert) Churchyard, YKS.*

**SYMONDS** Pte. John James 3877 3rd/5th Batt. West Yorkshire Regt. (Prince of Wales's Own). Died 11th March 1916 age 29. Son of Daniel and Emma Symonds, of Greentree, Shrimpling, Bury St. Edmunds.

*Source - CWGC/Bur. St. Alban's Churchyard, Forest Town. NTT.*

**WADDINGTON** Cpl. A V, 35677 5th Inf. Labour Coy. Lincolnshire Regiment transf. to (25878) 377th Home Service Coy. Labour Coy. Labour Corps. Died 5th December 1918 age 31. Husband of E R Waddington, of 170 Ashville Rd., Grove Green Rd., Leytonstone, LDN.

*Source - CWCG/ Bur. St. Alban's Churchyard, Forest Town. NTT.*

**WELLS** Pte. Frederick Charles 126429 3rd Batt. Machine Gun Corps (Inf). Died 2nd January 1918 age 19.

*Source - CWGC/StAlban's Burial Register/Bur. St. Alban's Churchyard, Forest Town. NTT.*

**WILSON** Cpl. William Henry 343793 Durham Light Infantry transf. to Labour Corps. Died of pneumonia 3rd June 1918 age 40 in Clipstone Camp Hospital. Eldest Son of John Wilson, cabinet maker and upholsterer of Blenavon Cottage, Yarm, YKS, and the late Elizabeth Wilson. Born at Stockton-on-Tees, and enlisted there in Oct 1914 while living in Yarm.

*Source - CWGC/web sites re 'The War Dead of Yarm'/Bur. St. Alban's Churchyard, Forest Town. NTT*

**YOUNG** Nurse, Ada Elizabeth, Voluntary Aid Detachment. Died 15th July 1918 of Influenza, Pneumonia and Cardiac Failure age 33. Daughter of the late Sjt. Maj. Young (5th Dragoon Guards) and Mrs. Young of Dublin.

*Source - CWGC/Death Certificate/Bur. S. Alban's Churchyard, Forest Town. NTT.*

# SELECTED BIBLIOGRAPHY

Bourne  J M            *Britain & The Great War 1914-18,* (1989)
Bristow  Philip        *The Mansfield Brew,* (Ringwood Hants. 1976)
Brittain Vera          *Testament of Youth* (2004)
Brown Malcolm          *The Imperial War Museum Book of The First World War* (1991)
Brown H W              *Mansfield's Co-operative Advance 1864-1950* (Manchester 1950)
Crute D                *Mansfield: The Last Century - The Industrial Development of Mansfield Since 1981,* (Nottingham 1991)
Emden Richard van & Humphries Steve
                       *All Quiet on the Western Front* (2003)
Fareham  J C           *Clipstone Camp*
Foley Michael          *As Hard As Nails, The Sportsmen's Battalion of World War One -* (Gloucestershire 2007)
Jackson Michael J      *A Shining Light - A History of Bridge Street Chapel* (Nottingham 2002 )
James E A              *British Regiments* 1914-1918 (1978)
Gamble T               *Court in Time* (Nottingham 1999)
Griffin A R            *Mining in the East Midlands, 1550-1947* (1971),
Honeybone M            *Book of Grantham, The History of a Market and Manufacturing Town,* (Buckingham 1980)
Markham D.             *Nottingham and the Great War* (University of Nottingham, Centre for Local History 1984)
Marples Pauline        *Mansfield and the Impact of The Great War,* Thesis University of Nottingham 1997
Marwick  A             *Women at War 1914-1918,* (1977)
Marwick Arthur         *Britain in the Century of Total War - War and Peace Total Change 1900 - 1967* (Middlesex 1968)
Marwick Arthur          *The Deluge: British Society and the First World War 2nd Edition,* (1971)
Noble  J               *Extracts from St John's School Log Book 1859-1950.*
Portland Duke of       *Men, Women and Things,* (1937)
Putkowoski J           *The Kimnel Camp Riots* (Clywd 1989)
Simkins P              *Kitchener's Army,* (Manchester 1988)
Stevenson & Woodward
                       *The First Hundred Years* (Notts 1995)
Taylor A J P           *English History 1914-1945,* (Oxford 1965)

Tiller Kate            Remembrance And Community: War Memorials And Local History (Derbys. 2013)
Watson J                *Success in British History Since 1914* (1983)
Winter Jay & Blaine Baggett
                       *1914-18 The Great War and the Shaping of the 20th Century (1996)    The War Graves Of The British Empire, Cemeteries and Churchyards in Nottinghamshire* (1930)
Not stated             *The History Of The Royal Fusiliers "UPS" University And Public Schools Brigade* (1917)
                       *A Celebration of Kings Clipstone* 1000 Years of History
                       *WW1 Diary of James Lee* [unpublished]

## SELECTED WEB SITES

www. britishnewspaperarchive.co.uk
www.cwcg.org
www.london-gazette.co.uk
www.nationalarchives.gov.uk
www.findmypast.co.uk

## GENERAL INDEX

### A

Absent Voters, 123
Accident(s), 57, 79, 95, 96,116
Accidental death, 38
Accommodation, 3, 26, 35, 39, 45, 59, 61, 63, 76, 77, 97, 102, 119
Active citizens, 128
Administration block, 35
Advertisements, 9, 24, 35, 117, 119
Aeroplane munitions factory, 89
Aeroplanes, 85
Age minimum/limit, 11
Agricultural land, 22, 87
**Agriculture**, 89
Centre at Welbeck, 89, 90
Notts. University College, 89
Ambulance wagon, 27
**Ammunition.**
Box(es), 15,73
Box Maker, 15
Annual Reports, 22, 23, 78
Armed Forces, 75
Armistice, 112, 113
Armistice Day, 125
**Army**, 1, 2, 3, 4, 8, 9,10, 11, 12, 13,49, 61, 75, 91, 98, 101, 113,119, 125, 128
Cadet Corps, 83
Camp, 129
Contracts, 24, 112, 115
Nursing Service, 106
Reserve, 17
Service Corps, 28, 112, 115
Artefacts, 125
Autograph book, 46, 48, 94, 129

### B

Bad women, 69
Bags of straw, 33, 45

Bank Holiday
Monday, 64
**Banks**, 35
Barclays, 35
London City & Midland, 35
**Barracks.**
construction, 25
Normanton, 115
**Bathing**, 63
Parade, 43
Piquet, 44
**Battalion(s)**, 8, 12, 26, 32, 45, 50, 59, 63, 64, 66, 68, 114, 128
**Battles.**
Jutland, 78
Neuve Chapelle, 83
Somme, 78
Bayonet(s), 33, 45, 67
Belgian/ people refugees, 73, 76, 131
**Bishop of**
Birmingham, 68
Sheffield, 39
Southwell, 34, 68
Bismarck Street, 128,
Blue Triangle, 97, 102
Boathouse, 44
Boilermakers, 10
Bolsover Colliery, 4, 12, 21, 28, 74, 75, 119
Boom Week, 85
Borough Surveyor, 82
Boxing Day, 50
Boys Brigade, 7
Bread Store, 36
Bricklayers, 35
Brigade, 7, 27, 37, 44, 45, 49, 59, 64
Britain, 2, 3, 5, 7, 13, 57, 87, 125, 131
Britain's population, 5
British Army, 1, 2
British Medical Journal, 88
Bugle(s), 30, 57
Bullets, 73
Bunks, 67
Burial, 57, 58
**Businesses**, 130
Alcock & Co. (Factory), 16
Blytheman Bros., 119
Boalers, 25

Bradley Ltd, 16
Bradley & Sons, 25
Bradwell & Sons, 119
Brewery, 130
Cooper Ltd, 34
Co-op, 16
Eastwoods, 119
Harwood Cash, 16
Hermitage Mill, 16, 76
Hodson and Sons, 25
Hollins & Co, 16
Moss Bros., 35
Player and Sons, 34
Shoe Co, 16
Wright of Woodhouse, 119
William Lawrence 89

### C

Cadet Company, 7
Cadet Corps, 66
**Camp**, 3
huts, 122
map, 35
new camp, 23, 27
open day, 59
sale, 117
site(s), 21, 23, 50
tent(s)d, 3, 4, 28, 45, 59, 114
**Canadian.**
Army, 67
Companies, 67
Ensign, 67
Forestry Lumber Jacks, 75
Remounts, 3
Candles, 27
Canvas, 3, 21, 28, 45
Carpenters, 35
Casualties, 63, 75
Casualty clearing stations, 92
Catalogue(s), 121, 122
Catering staff, 96
Celebrations, 73, 112
**Cemetery /
Churchyards**, 57, 58, 106, 116, 126
Bratton Baptist Chapel, 116

Fullham Palace, London, 116
Hill Top Leeds, 116
Mansfield, 116, 127
Nottingham, 53
Sighthill, 116
Sighthill Eastwood, Glasgow, 116
St Alban's, 116
St Helen's Pinxton, 116
St Mark's Cromford, 116
Cenotaphs, 125, 131
Census, 88
Chamber of Commerce, 67
Chapels, 50, 93
Children, 10, 13, 15, 34, 57, 68, 69, 76, 82, 87, 95, 98, 112, 119, 126
Chlorinating Plant, 22
Christmas, 1, 50, 51, 57, 82, 108
**Churches**, 34, 39, 50, 68, 93, 122
Church Mission Forest Town, 93
St Alban's Church, 34, 106, 122, 127
St George the Martyr, 34
Committee, 58
Civil engineering, 74
Civilian population, 1, 59
Civvy street, 113
Clerks, 10
Clipstone Camp, 5, 17, 21, 22, 23, 24, 26, 27, 28, 29, 30, 31, 33, 35, 38, 39, 42, 43, 45, 46, 49, 53, 54, 57, 59, 60, 62, 63, 65, 67, 68, 69, 70, 74, 78, 79, 80, 81, 82, 83, 84, 85, 90, 93, 95, 96, 97, 98, 101, 102, 103, 104, 105, 106, 107, 108, 110, 111, 112, 113, 114, 115, 116, 117, 118, 119, 120, 121, 125, 126, 127, 128, 129, 130, 131

## PLACE INDEX

**A**

Aberdeen, 49
Aldershot, 1, 21
Alexandria, 91
Alfreton, 59
America, 74
Annesley, 84
Aston Villa, 64
Aylesbury, 106

**B**

Bagthorpe, 53
Battenberg, 9
Bauchi Province, 127
Bedfordshire, 30
Beeston, 34
Belgium, 13, 91, 131
Belton Camp, 68
Birmingham, 68, 91
Bismarck Street, 128
Blackwell, 59
Bleasby, 2
Bolsover, 4, 12, 21, 28, 59, 74, 75, 76, 120
Bradford, 38, 50, 128
Bramshott, 21
Brighton, 64
Britain, 2, 7
Brockton Camp, 24
Buckingham Palace, 1

**C**

Cambridge, 64
Charloeroi, 76
Chatham, 49
China, 127
Clapton Orient, 64
Clipstone, 4, 5, 17, 21, 22, 23, 24, 25, 26, 27, 28, 29, 30, 31, 33, 35, 37, 38, 39, 42, 43, 45, 46, 49, 50, 52, 53, 54, 57, 59, 60, 62, 63, 65, 67, 68, 69, 70, 74, 75, 78, 79, 80, 81, 82, 83, 84, 85, 90, 93, 95, 96, 97, 98, 101, 102, 103, 104, 105, 106, 107, 108, 110, 111, 112, 113, 114, 115, 116, 117, 118, 119, 120, 121, 122, 123, 125, 126, 127, 128, 129, 130, 131
Clipstone Camp, 5, 21, 24, 27, 69, 70, 83, 98, 106, 107, 112, 113, 120, 126, 128, 131
Coal Aston, 112
Colston Bassett, 89
Colwick, 89
Cranwell, 115
Crich Stand, 39
Cromford, 116
Crown Farm, 28
Crown Farm Colliery, 43
Croydon Common, 64
Cuckney, 84

**D**

Dardinelles, 92
**Derby**, 28, 35, 111, 112, 115, 120, 123
    Burton Rd, 112
    Normanton Barracks, 115
    Tenant Street, 120
Derbyshire, 8, 13, 39, 76, 116
Donnington, 112
Dublin, 106

**E**

East Yorks, 113
Edwinstowe, 4, 27, 69, 84, 103, 115
Egypt, 82, 83, 114
England, 13, 30, 49, 83, 88, 101, 114
Epsom, 27
Essex, 30, 80
Exeter, 64

**F**

Farnsfield, 84, 115

**Forest Town**, 7, 12, 13, 21, 22, 23, 24, 27, 28, 29, 34, 45, 57, 63, 64, 66, 67, 79, 82, 84, 93, 101, 106, 112, 116, 120, 123, 126, 127
    First Avenue, 123
Fovant, 21
France, 30, 43, 68, 83, 91, 92, 101, 103, 114, 126, 128

**G**

Genappe, 76
Germany, 1, 7, 13, 73
Glasgow, 49, 116
Golf Club House, 123
Gombi, 127
Grand Theatre, 68, 102
Grantham, 68, 69, 115
Great Britain, 3, 7
Grimsby, 74

**H**

Halam, 2
Halifax, 50
Hants, 64
Harlow Wood, 122
Hermitage Mill, 76
Hong Kong, 127
Huddersfield, 64
Hull, 128
Hunmanby, 8
Huthwaite, 52

**I**

Immingham, 74, 75
Italy, 114

**J**

Jutland, 78

**K**

Kegworth, 112
Kinmel Park, 21
Kirkby, 2, 74

**L**

Le Havre, 114
Lancaster, 53, 120
Lancs, 66
Langwith, 84
Larkhill, Perham Down, 21
Leeds, 116
Leicester, 112, 113, 115
Lichfield, 24, 115
Lincoln, 77, 78, 90, 115
Lincolnshire Scotter, 123
Liverpool, 64
London, 2, 7, 9, 35, 36, 63, 74, 76, 82, 89, 103, 105, 106, 114, 116
Tilbury Docks, 114
Trafalgar Square, 7
Loughborough, 35, 89

**M**

Malta, 91
**Mansfield**, 1, 4, 5, 7, 8, 9, 10, 11, 12, 13, 14, 15, 16, 17, 21, 22, 23, 24, 25, 26, 27, 28, 29, 30, 33, 34, 38, 43, 50, 52, 53, 57, 58, 59, 60, 61, 62, 63, 64, 66, 67, 68, 69, 70, 72, 73, 74, 75, 76, 77, 78, 79, 80, 81, 82, 83, 84, 85, 87, 88, 89, 90, 91, 92, 93, 94, 95, 96, 97, 98, 99, 101, 102, 103, 108, 111, 112, 113, 115, 116, 117, 118, 119, 120, 121, 122, 123, 125, 126, 127, 128, 129, 130, 131
    Bath Lane, 7
    Belvedere Street, 123
    Bridge St, 80, 93
    Carr Bank Park, 131

**SURNAME INDEX**

**A**

Acton, 52
Alexander, 116
Alvey, 82
Argles, 1, 4, 17, 63
Atkinson, 114
Avond, 76

**B**

Badley, 80
Baggaley, 62
Bailey, 64
Bainbridge, 91
Baker, 64
Ball, 52
Balydon, 90
Barber, 64
Barnfather, 64
Battenberg, 9
Baxter, 102, 103
Beadsmoore, 114
Bean, 96, 107
Behagg, 39
Bell, 116
Bentinck, 84, 89, 91,
    92, 97, 102, 131
Bevis, 34
Birks, 93, 115
Bismarck, 128
Blythman, 119, 120
Boalers, 25
Boole, 15
Bosworth, 115
Bourne, 87
Bradley, 16, 25
Brailsford, 103
Brameld, 80
Bray, 128
Brew, 58
Brocklebank, 2
Brookes, 69
Brooks, 89, 103
Brown, 2
Bull, 106
Bullock, 64
Bunting, 34
Buxton, 34

**C**

Carding, 2
Castle, 68
Chadwick, 48, 94
Chesshire, 32
Churchill, 1

Clarke, 58
Coates, 52
Cockcroft, 69, 103
Coleman, 64
Collins, 68
Cooper, 34
Cox, 115
Coxhead, 52
Cregan, 68
Croucher, 52
Cumberland, 115
Cutts, 57

**D**

Davis, 53
Dean, 98
Dodsley, 115
Draper, 98
Driffill, 17
Dunstan, 46

**E**

Edwards, 106
Ellis, 13

**F**

Fairweather, 52
Fareham, 38
Featherstone, 127
Finney, 114
Flemming, 59
Footit, 52
Foster, 2, 64
Frost, 68
Fuller, 83

**G**

Gadd, 82
Garside, 53
Gibson, 64
Gillott, 53
Gilmour, 59
Gladstone Short, 57
Goodman, 123
Goodwin, 64
Gorton, 63
Green, 69, 98
Gregory, 64
Grewcock, 69, 103
Griffin, 75
Griffiths, 67

**H**

Haldane, 1, 2

Hall, 94
Hallam, 115
Hamilton, 49
Hammond, 91
Hampshire, 123
Hansen, 46
Harris, 52, 66
Harvey, 94
Havenhand, 57
Head, 15, 96
Henrick, 52
Hickling, 2
Hill, 68
Hodson, 25
Hogarth, 114
Holding, 107
Hotson, 82
Houfton, 12, 13, 21,
    57, 74, 75, 76, 89,
    91, 95, 115
Hudson, 58
Hugall, 64
Hume-Williams, 29
Hunt, 69, 98
Husskison, 82
Hutchinson, 123

**J**

Jagger, 16
James, 2
Jeoffcock, 11
Jones, 52, 64, 90

**K**

King, 77
Kirton, 66
Kitchener, 2, 3, 8, 9,
    10, 11, 21, 35
Knighton, 52

**L**

Lambie, 88
Lancaster, 120
Lewin, 2
Linton, 58
Lock, 69, 103
Longhurst, 106

**M**

Maclean, 103
Manvers, 76
Markham, 91, 98
Marlow, 115
Marshall, 98
Marwick, 87, 90

Mason, 90, 123
Maxwell, 67
Mee, 94
Megson, 128
Mildred, 90
Moss, 35
Munnings, 57
Murray, 63

**N**

Newton, 28
Nicholls, 105, 106

**O**

Orridge, 58
Osler, 79
Ovens, 106
Owen, 68

**P**

Parker, 17
Pearce, 91
Pearson, 52, 67, 68
Peel, 93
Percival, 106
Plant, 52
Player, 34
Portland, 8, 9, 12,
    21, 34, 35, 50, 67,
    68, 84, 87, 89, 91,
    92, 95
Pott, 107
Proudlove, 97

**R**

Redfern, 94
Rhodes, 52
Richardson, 53
Riley, 119
Roberts, 82
Robinson, 52

**S**

Samuel, 102
Sandilands, 127
Savidge, 57
Saville, 52
Scott, 64
Sealy, 84
Sheldon, 64
Shelmerdine, 95, 96
Simpson, 66
Slater, 92
Smith, 15, 81, 123